# ALLEN JOHNSON

# NIGHTSONG

Alto Saxophone in E♭

ED 3992

First Printing: June 1996

ISBN 978-0-7935-5699-1

# G. SCHIRMER, Inc.

DISTRIBUTED BY

HAL•LEONARD®
CORPORATION

7777 W. BLUEMOUND RD. P.O. BOX 13819 MILWAUKEE, WI 53213

**Alto Saxophone
in E♭**

# NIGHTSONG

Allen Johnson

# Vibrato

Jaw vibrato:  B = o = _____

more breath  B = o = ♩ ♩ ♩ ♩
～～～～～～

= ♫ ♫ ♫ ♫
～～～～～～

3
♫♫

♫♫

Cantabile - singing style

# ALLEN JOHNSON

# NIGHTSONG

ED 3992

First Printing: June 1996

ISBN 978-0-7935-5699-1

## G. SCHIRMER, Inc.

DISTRIBUTED BY

HAL•LEONARD®
CORPORATION

7777 W. BLUEMOUND RD. P.O. BOX 13819 MILWAUKEE, WI 53213

## Instrumentation

Solo Alto Saxophone in E♭

2 Flutes
Oboe
2 Clarinets in B♭
2 Bassoons

2 Horns in F
Trumpet in B♭
Trombone
Tuba

Bells
Harp

Strings

*Duration: ca. 5 minutes*

*Premiere performance: April 13, 1989, Maryville College, Maryville, Tennessee, Kenneth Radnofsky, saxophone*

**Performance material is available on rental from the publisher.**

*to Kenneth Radnofsky*

# NIGHTSONG

Allen Johnson

ossia: ottava sopra al fine

# The MAYNE

**Mark Hughes** CMILT

## Venture *publications*

*Front cover:* This East Lancs-bodied Scania demonstrates the striking and attractive livery which helped Mayne's vehicles to stand out in the city. *(JAS)*

*Above:* GNF 816E was one of six Bedford VAM14s with Plaxton Panorama coachwork delivered in March 1967. *(PM)*

*Facing:* Volvo B9R/Plaxton Elite number 14 was originally YX14 SEY before becoming MA14 YNE in April 2019. *(Mayne)*

*Rear cover:* This 1965 AEC Regent V is pictured in Dale Street in Manchester, on the original fast service to Audenshaw. *(AC)*

Backbone of the bus fleet in the 1990s were 12 former London Fleetlines. Number 34, THX 594S, entered service in the summer of 1991 and was operated until March 1998. *(JAS)*

# CONTENTS

# ACKNOWLEDGEMENTS

Photos were kindly supplied by Brian Lomas (BL), Howard Wilde (HW) and Phil Mott (PM), with additional material from the authors collection (AC), Reg Davis (RD), David Barrow (DB), Dave Farrier (DF), Geoff Lumb (GL), Greater Manchester Transport Society (GMTS), Liz Hall (LH), Peter Henson (PH), Roy Marshall (RM), the late Harry Postlethwaite (HSP), Peter Scott (PS) and John Senior (JAS).

I am grateful to them for their help, as well as for the generous assistance provided by Gradyn Thompson, Rob Vernon, Chris and Andrew Mayne, Amanda Jackson, David Yarwood, Eric Sutcliffe, Julian Peddle, John and Mark Senior, plus Graham Ashworth, and the late Olive and Stephen Mayne, Tommy Proctor and Peter Deegan, who helped with the original publication in 1995.

This book is dedicated with enormous gratitude to my late father, Victor Hughes, for encouraging a young boy's strange interest in a small bus and coach company.

Mark Hughes,
October 2022.

# THE MAYNE WAY

**M**emories were made on a Mayne's. For many years this much-admired family business was Manchester's oldest and only independent bus operator. They had a loyal following and were something special to those who worked or regularly travelled on their distinctive vehicles.

After being formed to deliver furniture in 1920, the firm went on to introduce the first regular coach service from East Manchester to Blackpool and provided alternative local transport during the General Strike in 1926. Realising the potential, Mayne continued running buses along Ashton New Road, much to the annoyance of Manchester Corporation, who tried to put an end to their activities.

Having fought hard to win licences in the 1930's, the family concern capitalised on the travel boom that followed the second world war, taking over several coach firms, including Barry Cooper Coaches of Warrington in 1982.

Their bus operation meanwhile outlasted the municipal trams and trolleybuses and continued through the era of Greater Manchester Transport. They grew and thrived after deregulation in 1986 until rising costs and car ownership finally caught up with them in 2008.

Mayne Coaches continued, however, to reach its centenary in 2020, before the devastating impact of the Coronavirus pandemic led to its sale after 102 years of operation. This book tells the story of this remarkable operator and the changing times of the towns and people they served.

## ABOUT THE AUTHOR

Mark Hughes travelled on Mayne's vehicles from a young age and his fascination with them led to a career in transport that's lasted over 30 years. This book, which began as a school assignment when Mark was just 14, was first published to mark the firm's 75th anniversary in 1995. It has since been re-written and updated with more information on the origins of this remarkable business, its coach operation and, of course, the buses that are still fondly remembered by many today.

*Below: Mark's first book was published in 1995 to celebrate the Company's 75th Anniversary.*

The Mayne livery suited the former Greater Manchester Transport buses. Number 18 is seen in Mossley in July 1987. *(BL)*

Mayne were soon operating a smart fleet of new Scania buses, including a pair of long-wheelbase examples (R108/9 YBA) delivered in 1997. *(PM)*

# CHAPTER 1: PIONEERS

There will always be something special about Mayne's. In the days before most families had cars, their buses and coaches enabled people to travel to school, work and even the seaside. The family business earned a reputation for reliability and had a loyal following, with many people still holding fond memories of travelling on their distinctive vehicles.

The founder, Arthur Mayne, was born in Salford on 20th May 1873. He was the youngest of George and Mary Mayne's eleven children and was raised in very humble circumstances. Like many Victorians, Arthur had to find work from an early age and was initially a barefoot newsboy, where salesmanship and ingenuity were needed to sell newspapers on the harsh cobbled streets. Most of his family worked in the furniture trade but Arthur was unemployed by the age of 17 and decided to join the Army.

It was while on leave in 1894 that he met 19 year-old Matilda Billing who was collecting donations for the local church. Smitten by her charm and determination, the 21-year-old soldier asked her out and ended up following her from pub-to-pub until she eventually agreed. They got married on 23rd March 1895 and Arthur obtained his discharge from the Manchester Rifles two months later. After moving to Clayton in east Manchester, Arthur started repairing furniture from their home at 27 Boardman Street - one of 14 terrace dwellings that housed 26 families, mostly in single rooms.

The street lay in the shadow of the power station chimneys and was later demolished to enable the adjacent aniline works to expand. There was also an enormous colliery and famous iron works where the Etihad Stadium stands today. Thousands worked there or in the local mills and factories, producing goods for export all over the world.

The saying goes that 'behind every successful man there is a wise woman', something Matilda would prove as their enterprise began selling drapes and other household furnishings. They opened a shop at 22 Wellington Street in neighbouring Beswick in 1903, later moving to larger premises in 1906, as their venture and family grew.

Their new store at 193 Ashton New Road was not far from the pit entrance, on a bustling thoroughfare linking Manchester with the more rural textile districts of Droylsden and Audenshaw, and the mill town of Ashton-under-Lyne. The couple lived in the rooms above the shop with their children - Arthur, Matilda, Alice, Olive and Lena.

Matilda Emily Mayne, seen below left, was the driving force behind several businesses and ran a furniture dealers and hardware business under her own name for many years. Born in Mossley on 4th August 1875, Matilda was the daughter of Robert and Louisa Billing, who were saddle and leather workers from Wisbech in Cambridge.

The Mayne family in 1917 (from back row) - Tilly, Arthur (junior), Alice, Arthur (senior), Olive, Lena and Matilda.

# FROM FURNITURE TO DAY TRIPS

Arthur Mayne (junior) was born on 10th September 1895. Although he was a quiet, unassuming lad, he enjoyed playing football, learnt to box, and was a member of both the Scouts and St John's Ambulance Brigade. He began an apprenticeship with his father as an upholsterer in 1909 and may also have worked with his uncles, George and Henry, in a furniture-making business known as the Mayne Brothers.

When war intervened, the 18-year-old joined the Royal Army Medical Corps, where he would learn something of motors, with some of the first Daimler and Ford ambulances. Its East Lancs Territorial division comprised of the 2nd Western Hospital and three field ambulance units that saw service in southern England, Egypt and the Western Front.

The base hospital was a requisitioned school on Whitworth Street in Manchester that, along with 22 auxiliary sites, cared for more casualties than any other in the country, with over 250,000 beds under its command by 1918. Arthur, who was a Corporal and a medical orderly by then, would unfortunately suffer the effects of poison gas whilst removing contaminated dressings from a casualty in July. He also later caught pneumonia. Gradually nursed back to better health, he was discharged from the Army on 9th May 1919.

Doctors advised him not to return to the furniture trade as the sawdust and toxins could affect his damaged lungs. The 25 year-old tried to make a go of it, but it soon became clear that an outside job was needed. His parents encouraged him to pursue his interest in motors and a Ford T was purchased in 1920 to transport goods and furniture in place of their horse, Dobbin. The Maynes had three shops by now, including a furniture store on the parallel Ashton Old Road and a drapery in West Gorton, run by Arthur's sister, Tilly. There was therefore plenty of work for the delivery van which was soon joined by surplus Army lorries that could carry greater payloads.

Arthur (junior) had by now fallen for Harriett Taylor, who everyone knew as 'Biddy'. The 26-year-old managed Matilda's accounts and would help him to develop the new venture and run the office. They would get married in January 1923 and move nearby to 48 Howarth Street. The Ford was garaged in the yard adjoining the property with at least one Dennis 4-tonne lorry parked outside.

An invitation followed to join a local co-operative involving James Ferrington's Pioneer Motors of Moston and Thomas Bryan's Premier Motors of Higher Openshaw, who worked with the steam waggon operator George Leggott & Son

Corporal Arthur Mayne (junior) served in the Royal Army Medical Corps from 1914 to 1919. *(LH)*

Arthur's first wife, Harriett, who was known as Biddy, was born in Salford on 9th December 1896. The daughter of John and Sarah Taylor, she may also have been a cousin of the Mayne's neighbours, Fred and Nellie Taylor, who ran a music shop at 195 Ashton New Road . Bid was the company's book-keeper until her untimely death on 9th April 1945, aged just 48. *(LH)*

Arthur's sister Tilly and her husband, Peter Beswick, ran a drapers and hardware shop at 155 Gorton Lane, West Gorton for many years. It was also a Mayne sales agent and pick-up point by 1929. Alice Mayne is seen here, possibly with one of Tilly and Peter's three children, alongside a blackboard advertising the service to Blackpool. The Beswick's would go on to run a hardware shop in Cheadle. *(Mayne family)*

of Clayton. This enabled them to share loads and cover a much larger area. Further lorries were purchased, including an AEC Y-Type and a Halford or Belsize (registration, NA 9673). Like the Ford and Dennis, they were capable of being converted to carry passengers at weekends.

Day trips and visits to race meetings had begun by May 1920, eventually increasing to four pick-up points along Ashton New Road by 1923 utilising licenses issued by Manchester Corporation. The family's shops and other local shopkeepers helped advertise the excursions and act as booking agents. The novelty of the open road clearly appealed to the public, as there was soon a demand for more from organisers of church and work outings.

Two motor coaches - an AEC 416 (TW 634) and a smaller AEC 509 (TW 1834) - were purchased in 1925 and the growing fleet was now garaged on land on the corner of Ashton New Road and Grey Mare Lane. Three more pick-up points were introduced in Beswick, along with the first regular coach service to Blackpool, serving Ashton-under-Lyne, Audenshaw, Droylsden, Clayton and Beswick. Despite initially taking three and a half hours to complete the 56-mile journey, the summer service was an immediate success.

## PIONEER BUSES

When the General Strike brought the City's trams to a halt in May 1926, the Pioneer consortium, along with several others, stepped in to provide services for the public. Realising the potential, many carried on running, despite being refused a permanent licence.

What is thought to be Mayne's Ford T in West Gorton in the 1920s. It had an interchangeable body system, allowing the chassis to be fitted with a box van for deliveries and, later, a saloon for carrying people. Fords were made in Trafford Park from 1911 until a larger facility was opened in Dagenham in 1931. (AC)

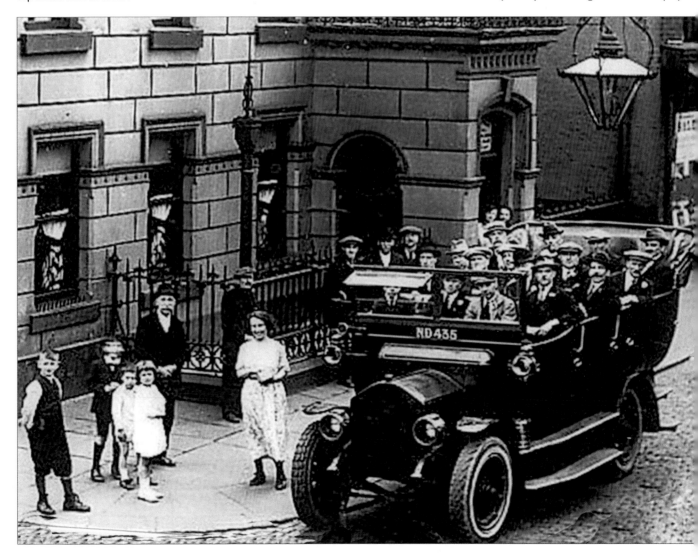

Another Pioneer outing, ready to depart with a group of children whose fathers had made the ultimate sacrifice in the First World War. Led by a Dennis 4-ton lorry (NA 9763) with a hastily transferred RAF-type charabanc body much favoured in the Leggott fleet. The two vehicles behind are in Mayne's maroon livery and are the Belsize lorry (NA 9673), with the AEC Y-Type at the rear. James Ferrington served in the Manchester Regiment, whose 24th Battalion were known as the Pioneers. *(Mayne/AC)*

Confusingly similar registration NA 9673 is thought to be a 3-tonne Belsize or Halford lorry. Belsize was a prolific manufacturer of cars and commercial vehicles from 1906-14 and named after the former bicycle works it occupied on Clayton Lane. After production switched to wartime munitions in 1916, Belsize struggled to revert back to vehicle manufacturing after the war and ceased trading in 1925. *(Mayne/AC)*

James Ferrington eventually obtained one from the fiercely independent Droylsden Urban District Council, enabling Pioneer to run from the town's Market Street junction from 14th November 1927. Possibly operated with Mayne's and Premier Motors' support, the service charged similar fares to the trams but provided a much quicker alternative. Still unlicensed within the City of Manchester, it terminated at Hilton Street garage, which was on private land and outside the Corporation's reach.

The City introduced its own motor buses to try and see off the threat to its tramway. Having started an express service between Clayton and Manchester on 18th October 1927, they eventually settled on a route between Ashton, Manchester, Chorlton and Urmston that was run with the help of Ashton-under-Lyne Corporation from 30th January 1928. The privately-owned North Western Road Car Company joined them when their Glossop to Stalybridge service was extended to Manchester on 1st March. The routes later merged in 1929, becoming service 6 between Glossop and Chorlton a year later.

Pioneer meanwhile had introduced three Crossley Eagle single-deckers in 1928 (VM 6225-7), running on a 15-minute frequency, widening to every half hour at quieter times. James also tried to run the dark-blue buses to Stretford but its town council, now negotiating for a share in the municipal express buses, twice refused.

Manchester's Watch Committee, frustrated at the inability of its motor buses to dispose of the independents, directed the City Police to investigate the 'pirate' operators. This resulted in a spate of prosecutions in the winter of 1928, mostly for speeding and selling tickets on unlicensed services. The penalties imposed on 41-year-old James led him to sell his interest to the Mayne family in January 1929. He went on to establish North Manchester Motors in 1933, a joint venture that eventually became part of Yelloway in 1968.

## THE FIGHT FOR A LICENCE

Audenshaw Parish Council gave Arthur (junior) permission to extend the bus route from Droylsden to Kershaw Lane in March 1929. An AEC 660 Reliance bus (VR 498) soon replaced the Y-Type, resulting in the haulage work passing to the Leggott's, who would continue in business with a fleet of 26 vehicles for another decade.

Manchester Corporation rejected Mayne's application for a stage carriage licence on 8th February 1929 and an Appeal to the Minister for Transport in July failed to improve matters. Some 10,000 passengers were now using the service each week and they were encouraged to buy a return ticket. This ensured Mayne were not plying-for-hire within the city boundary. It also enabled them to extend the route to Piccadilly, much to the annoyance of the Watch Committee, who began questioning the renewal of Mayne's excursions licence in June 1930. They were still debating the matter when responsibility for licensing passed, under the Road Traffic Act 1930, to the Ministry of Transport and its regional Traffic Commissioners.

This "all-weather" Dennis motor coach probably came with the purchase of Thomas Bryan's Premier Motors operation and seen in Queen Street, Beswick. It was later modernised into a half-cab appearance, with a panelled roof and the addition of high-back seating for the Blackpool service. (Mayne/AC)

Operators now faced a daunting level of control where vehicles, drivers, conductors, services and fares would all be licensed and regulated. They would now have to prove there was a need for a service, excursion or tour. The local authority, police or even a competitor could object, enabling the application to be debated in a formal Traffic Court.

Mayne sought a stage carriage licence under this new system in April 1931, only to be denied after Manchester Corporation and North Western claimed the service was unnecessary. Arthur (junior) appealed the decision. With help from a barrister and the support of Droylsden Council, they later persuaded the North West Traffic Commissioner that the service was actually of great utility.

A licence was granted on 11th June 1932, with conditions attached that prevented the carriage of passengers travelling solely within Manchester. The service also had to observe limited stops within the City, charge ½d more than the trams and change its terminus. It was later agreed that it would terminate at 25 Dale Street, one block east of Piccadilly. The Aldermen, still unhappy, lodged an appeal, seeking further protection for the tramway but the decision was upheld - Mayne finally had a licence to run buses in Manchester.

VR 498 was acquired from the Associated Equipment Company's local distributor, Harold Rothwell, to aid the extension of the bus route to Kershaw Lane in 1929. The AEC 660 Reliance had a six-cylinder engine that had a propensity to kangaroo starts. Mayne's AEC 509, TW 1834, is at the rear. (Mayne/AC)

OUR NEW DENNIS CHARA will LEAVE MAYNE'S, House Furnisher, Ashton New Road, for the following places at time stated:—
KNUTSFORD, SATURDAY, May 1, 1920, 12.45.
CHESTER RACES on the 4th, 5th, and 6th, 9 a.m.
We still have MANY DATES OPEN for coming season.
4-TON PETROL WAGGONS CAN BE HAD AT ANY TIME.

A. MAYNE & SON, BESWICK.

# CHAPTER 2: MILESTONES

Shortly before the Road Traffic Act was introduced, Mayne acquired Premier Motors and consolidated the Pioneer fleets into new premises on Queen Street in Beswick. They were granted an excursions licence from 13th December 1931, with 12 pick-up points, despite objections from several operators and the London Midland & Scottish Railway.

Authorised to operate up to three departures a day, their seasonal destinations included Abergele (1 trip per season); Ambleside (1); Blackpool (54); Chester (7); Colwyn Bay (1); Hebden Bridge (1); Holcombe Brook (1); Keswick (1); Liverpool (2); Llandudno (2); Morecambe (7); Rhyl (3); Silverdale (1) and Southport (13).

The objectors did, however, succeed in preventing Mayne expanding into Salford and from starting the Blackpool service in Stalybridge. It was also limited to one vehicle and 220 departures a season, with the option of period return fares from 12th March 1932. A new AEC Regal coach (XJ 5574) was bought for the service in August 1933, joining two second-hand examples that replaced the maroon-coloured AEC's.

Despite making it into the new licensing system, privately-owned bus companies continued to clash with Manchester Corporation. Operators such as Cash, Goodfellow's, Organ and Wachter, Orr, Sharp, Syke Brothers and even Yelloway would all be persuaded to stop running buses, one way or another.

Having gained a reputation for reliability, Mayne were determined to benefit from plans to double Droylsden's population to 26,000 within 20 years. They applied to run a feeder route along Manor Road to connect with the existing service at Edge Lane in October 1932, utilising the first of four Dennis E-type single-deckers from Yorkshire Woollen & District. Manchester Corporation objected but the Traffic Commissioner, noting that the road was unserved, granted the licence from 21st January 1933. Plans for more journeys on the Audenshaw route were rejected, however, and a briefly implemented extension to Audenshaw (Snipe) Bridge, following Council concerns about reversing at Kershaw Lane was eventually dropped.

Arthur Mayne (senior), now aged 60, was a prominent member of Droylsden's Lodge of Freemasons and had been invited to stand as a local councillor on several occasions. Arthur took little interest in politics though, preferring to devote his spare time to his family, the Gospel Hall in Beswick, and following Lancashire County Cricket. He died on Sunday 17th September 1933 and was laid to rest in Droylsden Cemetery, alongside the family's new bus route on Manor Road.

This line-up, taken inside the Queen Street garage in 1930, features Crossley Eagle VM 6227, AEC Reliance VR 498, Dennis VM 1279 and AEC 509 TW 1834. The van body of the Ford is just visible in the background. *(Mayne/AC)*

The first covered garage on Queen Street was a former engineering works. It was just off Ashton New Road, close to Forge Lane (now Alan Turing Way) and later renamed Quinn Street. It survived as a hauliers and storage facility until the area was redeveloped as a football training campus in 2012. *(Mayne/AC)*

## THE REGENTS

Their first double-decker bus was delivered on 30th November 1934. AXJ 496 was an AEC Regent that had rather stylish Park Royal bodywork. The few hundredweight saved by fitting it with a petrol engine rather than a diesel, enabled it to seat 60 passengers inside. This was around eight more than most double-deckers of the time. Permission to use larger vehicles was obtained from 2nd June 1934, after Droylsden Council appealed the decision that had prevented Mayne from providing more journeys.

The Regent was also fitted with a small green light next to its destination display. This helped passengers identify the approaching vehicle during darkness, and in the regular episodes of smog that blighted industrial East Manchester. The feature was so successful that it was applied to all subsequent Mayne buses until 1957. It's most striking feature, however, was the distinctive and charismatic sound of its AEC engine.

This hurried shot, taken on a wet afternoon in Dale Street, was apparently an attempt to emphasise the double-decker's high capacity in comparison to the usual rear entrance models of the time. *(AEC/PRV)*

These photographs show the lower- and upper-deck interior. The severe limit on gross weights at the time meant that it was a little austere inside, although the absence of interior lining panels was not uncommon. The bus was regularly used on the Audenshaw and Blackpool routes and later fitted with an extra seat on each deck. This landmark vehicle was eventually retired in the summer of 1949. (AEC/PRV)

AXJ 496 is pictured on delivery on 30th November 1934. The AEC 661 Regent was built in Southall, London from 1929. Its bodywork was constructed by Park Royal Coach Works, later Park Royal Vehicles, with an unusual lightweight, forward-entrance design. (AEC/PRV)

An application was made in December 1934 to extend the Manor Road route to Chappell Road to assist workers at the Saxon Mill. Manchester again objected. The Traffic Commissioner remedied this by obtaining an agreement from Arthur that effectively confined the route within Droylsden from 2nd March 1935. Another AEC Regent arrived on 1st August. BNF 553 accommodated 62 passengers, making Arthur the proud owner of the highest-capacity two-axle bus in the country.

Once the probate of his father's estate was completed, the firm was registered under the Companies Act of 1929. A Mayne & Son Ltd was incorporated on 13th December 1935 with an initial share capital of £5,000. The registered address was the furniture shop at 193/5 Ashton New Road. Arthur and his mother, Matilda, were the directors and shareholders. There was also a furniture shop at 598 Gorton Road in Reddish, near Stockport, while Matilda owned hardware shops at 234 Ashton New Road and 592 Gorton Road. Other family enterprises included drapery shops run by Tilly, Lena and Alice in West Gorton, Reddish and Pendleton. Later there was also a hairdressing business run by Olive.

The bus routes earned £11,280 in 1935 and were clearly flourishing. The once rural Droylsden Road through Audenshaw also continued to develop with the building of new housing around Kershaw Lane. Mayne applied to serve the North Road estate (now North Drive) in February 1936, after Arthur bought a house for his mother on Lynwood Grove. They also proposed to run more journeys on Saturdays, but the Traffic Commissioner refused permission. Two more 62-seat Park Royal AEC Regents (CNB 1 and CVR 1) arrived in 1936, replacing the last of the Crossleys.

BNF 553, seen above right, was the highest capacity two-axle bus in the country in 1935 and joined by two more in 1936. It was damaged in the Blitz and rebuilt by East Lancashire Coachbuilders of Blackburn to a similar design in 1945, with a diesel engine and accommodation for 58 passengers. It was retired in March 1959 along with CNB 1. The last of the trio, CVR 1, seen below in Dale Street, was converted into a towing waggon in 1955. (Author's/BL)

# MORE LICENCE BATTLES

Although the Traffic Commissioner declined their application to acquire the Salford to Blackpool service of Lamb & Whittingslow, approval was given to purchase the excursions licence of DS Webb of 71 Ashton New Road, Beswick on 8th April 1936. Five more pick-up points were added in Clayton, mostly around North Road, bringing the total to 17. The authorised daily excursions rose to four, with destinations now including Cleveleys, Fleetwood, Kendal, Lytham St Annes and New Brighton via the new Mersey Tunnel.

Arthur had obtained approval to start the Blackpool service in Stalybridge from 1st September 1934 and to run extra journeys during August and the Illuminations, providing the combined quota of 274 trips was maintained. The service now operated daily from 1st March until 31st October, departing from Stalybridge at 0815, Ashton at 0830, Audenshaw at 0840, Droylsden at 0850, Clayton at 0855 and Beswick at 0900. It returned from Blackpool at 1900 hours (2100 during the Illuminations). There was also an extra return trip at 1230 on Saturdays for period return customers during the Ashton Wakes Week, August bank holiday and the Illuminations. Three new AEC Regals were purchased in 1937, bringing the total to five, with the AEC Regents also regular performers on the Blackpool route.

The use of double-deck buses was approved on Manor Road after 2100 hours on Saturdays from 24th July 1937, after demand began to exceed the capacity of the single-deckers - one of which was a pig-nosed Albion (SM 8353). Acquired the previous summer, the bus had its capacity reduced from 28 to 20 to legally enable it to be operated without a conductor. Two buses now provided a 7½-minute frequency at peak times, with one needed for the 15-minute service during the rest of the day. With no television for entertainment people travelled to the various pubs, clubs or cinemas along Ashton New Road or into 'town', making the evening journeys remarkably busy.

Waiting time on the Manchester service was reduced on Dale Street from 9th October, following complaints from the Chief Constable about congestion. Four double-deckers now provided the ten-minute service in the peak, with only two running off-peak every 20 minutes (three every 15 minutes on Saturdays), one after midnight until 0220; and one every 40 minutes on Sundays and Public Holidays. The fast service took 20 minutes or less from Audenshaw and 15 from Droylsden.

This timetable was effective from 9th October 1937 and required at least four buses in the peak periods, although duplicates were provided when necessary. (AC)

**A. MAYNE & SON LTD.**
195, ASHTON NEW ROAD.

EASt 0707.
DROylsden 1396.

**AUDENSHAW—MANCHESTER**
(Via DROYLSDEN)
**SERVICES.**

# TIME TABLE.

**MONDAYS to FRIDAYS.** — Audenshaw to Manchester.

| | a.m. | a.m. | a.m. | and | a.m. | a.m. | then | p.m. | p.m. | and | p.m. | p.m. | then | p.m. | p.m. | a.m. | a.m. | a.m. |
|---|---|---|---|---|---|---|---|---|---|---|---|---|---|---|---|---|---|---|
| KERSHAW LANE, Audenshaw | 5 40 | 6 35 | 6 57 | EVERY | 9 7 | 9 27 | EVERY | 5 7 | 5 17 | EVERY | 6 27 | 6 47 | EVERY | 11 7 | 11 27 | 12 30 | 1 30 | 2 20 |
| MARKET ST., Droylsden | 5 45 | 6 40 | 7 0 | TEN | 9 10 | 9 30 | TWENTY | 5 10 | 5 20 | TEN | 6 30 | 6 50 | TWENTY | 11 10 | 11 30 | 12 35 | 1 35 | |
| EDGE LANE, " | 5 50 | 6 45 | 7 4 | MINUTES | 9 14 | 9 34 | MINUTES | 5 14 | 5 24 | MINUTES | 6 34 | 6 54 | MINUTES | 11 14 | 11 34 | 12 45 | 1 45 | TO DEPOT |
| DALE STREET, Manchester | 6 0 | 6 55 | 7 17 | to | 9 27 | 9 47 | to | 5 27 | 5 37 | to | 6 47 | 7 7 | to | 11 30 | 11 55 | 1 0 | 2 0 | |

**MONDAYS to FRIDAYS.** — Manchester to Audenshaw.

| | a.m. | a.m. | a.m. | and | a.m. | then | p.m. | p.m. | and | p.m. | p.m. | then | p.m. | Midnight | a.m. | a.m. | |
|---|---|---|---|---|---|---|---|---|---|---|---|---|---|---|---|---|---|
| DALE STREET, Manchester | 6 0 | 7 5 | 7 17 | EVERY | 9 27 | EVERY | 5 0 | 5 15 | EVERY | 6 40 | 6 47 | EVERY | 11 30 | 12 0 | 1 0 | 2 0 | |
| EDGE LANE, Droylsden | 6 15 | 7 18 | 7 30 | TEN | 9 40 | TWENTY | 5 5 | 5 15 | TEN | 6 40 | 7 0 | TWENTY | 11 45 | 12 15 | 1 15 | | |
| MARKET ST. | 6 25 | 7 23 | 7 35 | MINUTES | 9 45 | MINUTES | 5 10 | 5 16 | MINUTES | 6 45 | 7 5 | MINUTES | 11 50 | 12 20 | 1 20 | | |
| KERSHAW LANE, Audenshaw | 6 30 | 7 25 | 7 37 | to | 9 47 | to | 5 7 | 5 17 | to | 6 47 | 7 7 | to | 11 55 | 12 30 | 1 30 | 2 20 TO DEPOT | |

**SATURDAYS.** — Audenshaw to Manchester.

| | a.m. | a.m. | a.m. | and | a.m. | a.m. | then | Noon | p.m. | and | p.m. | p.m. | p.m. | a.m. | |
|---|---|---|---|---|---|---|---|---|---|---|---|---|---|---|---|
| KERSHAW LANE, Audenshaw | 5 40 | 6 35 | 6 57 | EVERY | 9 7 | 9 27 | EVERY | 12 7 | 12 25 | EVERY | 11 25 | 12 30 | 1 30 | 2 20 | |
| MARKET ST., Droylsden | 5 45 | 6 40 | 7 0 | TEN | 9 10 | 9 30 | TWENTY | 12 10 | 12 27 | FIFTEEN | 11 30 | 12 35 | 1 35 | | |
| EDGE LANE, | 5 50 | 6 45 | 7 4 | MINUTES | 9 14 | 9 34 | MINUTES | 12 14 | 12 30 | MINUTES | 11 34 | 12 45 | 1 45 | TO DEPOT | |
| DALE STREET, Manchester | 6 0 | 6 55 | 7 17 | to | 9 27 | 9 47 | to | 12 30 | 12 45 | to | 11 55 | 1 0 | 2 0 | | |

**SATURDAYS.** — Manchester to Audenshaw.

| | a.m. | a.m. | a.m. | and | a.m. | then | Noon | p.m. | p.m. | p.m. | and | p.m. | p.m. | a.m. | a.m. | |
|---|---|---|---|---|---|---|---|---|---|---|---|---|---|---|---|---|---|
| DALE STREET, Manchester | 6 0 | 7 5 | 7 17 | EVERY | 9 27 | EVERY | 12 7 | 12 20 | 12 30 | 12 45 | EVERY | 11 30 | 12 0 | 1 0 | 2 0 | |
| EDGE LANE, Droylsden | 6 15 | 7 18 | 7 30 | TEN | 9 45 | MINUTES | 12 20 | 12 35 | 12 45 | 1 0 | FIFTEEN | 11 45 | 12 15 | 1 15 | | |
| MARKET ST. | 6 25 | 7 23 | 7 35 | MINUTES | 9 45 | MINUTES | 12 23 | 12 37 | 12 50 | 1 5 | MINUTES | 11 50 | 12 20 | 1 20 | | |
| KERSHAW LANE, Audenshaw | 6 30 | 7 25 | 7 37 | to | 9 47 | to | 12 30 | 12 40 | 12 53 | 1 10 | to | 11 55 | 12 30 | 1 30 | 2 20 TO DEPOT | |

**SUNDAYS.** — Audenshaw to Manchester.

| | a.m. | p.m. | p.m. | p.m. | p.m. | p.m. | p.m. | and | p.m. | p.m. | p.m. | p.m. | p.m. | |
|---|---|---|---|---|---|---|---|---|---|---|---|---|---|---|
| KERSHAW LANE, Audenshaw | 11 30 | 12 10 | 12 50 | 1 30 | 2 10 | 2 50 | 3 30 | EVERY | 9 50 | 10 10 | 10 50 | 11 10 | 11 30 | |
| MARKET ST., Droylsden | 11 32 | 12 12 | 12 52 | 1 32 | 2 12 | 2 52 | 3 32 | FORTY | 9 52 | 10 12 | 10 52 | 11 12 | 11 32 | |
| EDGE LANE, | 11 35 | 12 15 | 12 55 | 1 35 | 2 15 | 2 55 | 3 35 | MINUTES | 9 55 | 10 15 | 10 55 | 11 15 | 11 35 | |
| DALE STREET, Manchester | 11 50 | 12 30 | 1 10 | 1 50 | 2 30 | 3 10 | 3 50 | to | 10 10 | 10 30 | 10 50 | 11 10 | 11 30 | TO DEPOT |

**SUNDAYS.** — Manchester to Audenshaw.

| | a.m. | p.m. | p.m. | p.m. | p.m. | p.m. | p.m. | and | p.m. | p.m. | p.m. | p.m. | p.m. | |
|---|---|---|---|---|---|---|---|---|---|---|---|---|---|---|
| DALE STREET, Manchester | 11 50 | 12 30 | 1 10 | 1 50 | 2 30 | 3 10 | 3 50 | EVERY | 9 50 | 10 30 | 10 50 | 11 10 | 11 30 | |
| EDGE LANE, Droylsden | 12 5 | 12 45 | 1 25 | 2 5 | 2 45 | 3 25 | 4 5 | FORTY | 10 5 | 10 25 | 10 45 | 11 5 | 11 45 | |
| MARKET ST. | 12 7 | 12 47 | 1 27 | 2 7 | 2 47 | 3 27 | 4 7 | MINUTES | 10 7 | 10 27 | 10 47 | 11 7 | 11 47 | |
| KERSHAW LANE, Audenshaw | 12 10 | 12 50 | 1 30 | 2 10 | 2 50 | 3 30 | 4 10 | to | 10 10 | 10 30 | 10 50 | 11 10 | 11 50 TO DEPOT | |

# END OF THE LINE?

Relations with Manchester Corporation were never great, but Arthur was as good-humoured as he was determined. When they offered to buy his bus services in 1937, Arthur apparently remarked on the timely coincidence, as he was thinking of buying some of theirs!

An application to extend the Manor Road route into a new estate off Chappell Road, along with plans to use double-deckers throughout, went unopposed in December 1937. The extension would take place once Sunnyside Road was completed in the winter of 1938. An AEC Regent was purchased from Nottingham Transport (TV 735) and soon followed by another from Exeter (FJ 7821), with plans to have them re-bodied by Park Royal. They joined the four high-capacity Regents, plus the Reliance and Albion, with six buses required.

Although the East Manchester community was close-knit, there was a real divergence amongst them when it came to football. Both Manchester clubs had their formative years in the area, with City founded in West Gorton in 1880, and United playing in Clayton from 1893 until 1910. Having provided transport to home matches since 1923, Mayne obtained approval to run double-deck buses to Old Trafford or Maine Road on 15th January 1938, after an 11-month battle in the Traffic Courts.

Shortly afterwards, Manchester Corporation announced that it was to buy Mayne's bus operation on 25th March for £51,000 (around £2.4 million in today's money) and launch an experimental trolleybus service, but Arthur changed his mind. Annual revenue on the routes had now reached £14,800 - over 16d a mile and growing.

The excursions licence of John Bowker of 21 Cross Street, Bradford, Manchester, was acquired on 30th July along with a 1936 AEC Regal (BNF 773), although his remaining coach hire business continued into the 1950s. Bowker ran excursions to Blackpool and Southport from three pick-up points in Bradford and Beswick. The move coincided with the introduction of the Holidays with Pay Act that gave workers the right to one week's paid holiday a year, increasing the demand for coach travel. It also encouraged Mayne to try expanding further, despite talk of war following Germany's invasion of Austria. Applications to run excursions from Droylsden, Audenshaw, Ashton and Stalybridge were denied, however, following opposition from other local operators.

Manchester City Council decided to convert the tram routes along Ashton New Road and others to trolleybuses from 31st July 1938, leaving Mayne as the most frequent motor bus provider to Droylsden and Audenshaw. Over 500,000 passengers travelled on the buses that summer (around 38,000 a week) and a further 20,000 travelled on the excursions and Blackpool service, as day trips and memories continued to be made on a Maynes.

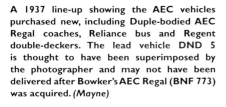

A 1937 line-up showing the AEC vehicles purchased new, including Duple-bodied AEC Regal coaches, Reliance bus and Regent double-deckers. The lead vehicle DND 5 is thought to have been superimposed by the photographer and may not have been delivered after Bowker's AEC Regal (BNF 773) was acquired. (Mayne)

# CHAPTER 3: SHORTAGES

By 1938, fitting the Regents inside the Queen St garage was a problem, despite alterations being made to get them inside. Fourteen drivers, ten conductors, an inspector, three mechanics and two cleaners were now employed, managed by Arthur's brother-in-law, Frank Wade. Despite starting to look for larger premises, work began on the roof to allow the double-deckers greater access to the inspection pit, only for a driver to accidentally drive straight into the building's exposed steel work with the newly re-bodied Nottingham Regent!

Arthur and Harriett were now living in Clayton at 865 Ashton New Road, near Seymour Road South. A dye-works and tannery was purchased nearby in January 1938 for around £3,000. A further £3,250 was spent converting the buildings into a booking office and waiting room, with an adjacent workshop that could accommodate four vehicles. There were also car repair facilities and a petrol forecourt, with land around it to park their 14 vehicles. The new headquarters at 974 Ashton New Road opened on 1st March 1939. Excursions had started there from 25th February, however, when their authorised daily departures increased to five. The Blackpool service also stopped there from 11th March, and at Hurst Cross in Ashton from 22nd July. The Queen Street depot was vacated on 13th May.

An AEC Regent new in 1931 with Brush bodywork was acquired from Exeter Corporation in 1938. FJ 7821 was intended to be re-bodied by Park Royal in 1939 but war intervened. East Lancashire Coachbuilders subsequently rebuilt it at a cost of £397 to a similar design to the early Park Royal examples in 1943. Seen in its wartime grey, the bus remained in service until 1960, by which time it was almost 30 years old. (RM)

A grainy image from a press cutting showing an AEC Regal trialling an Enness gas trailer in June 1940. The Duple-bodied coach was XJ 5574, new to Mayne in August 1933. It retained this method of propulsion until its retirement in 1953. Similar vehicle VH 3225, acquired from Hanson of Huddersfield in 1932, is also thought to have been converted but withdrawn from use in May 1947. (Commercial Motor/AC).

# THE WAR YEARS

Despite Prime Minister Chamberlain's attempts to secure 'peace for our time', Germany's aggression continued with the invasion of Czechoslovakia and then Poland, leading to war being declared on 3rd September 1939. Mayne's 1937 AEC Regals were commandeered by the military, never to return. Although the Blackpool service was suspended, limited excursions would continue until 1942.

As fuel restrictions increased, an AEC Regal (XJ 5574) was fitted with a 12cwt Enness Gas trailer in May 1940. The unit burned coke and when mixed with water vapour, reacted to form suction gas to run the vehicle's 110bhp petrol engine.

German troops had occupied France by June 1940 and Britain prepared for invasion. The Luftwaffe began a campaign of bombing ports and heavy industries, with Salford and Manchester being targeted from 29th July, in the 'Blitz'.

The raids intensified before Christmas 1940, when incendiary bombs, capable of melting steel, hit the Carlton Cinema and chemical works alongside the garage in Clayton. This caused fire and blast damage to at least three of the Regents, leading to the recruitment of firewatchers. Other streets, especially those near the power station, were much less fortunate, with dozens of terraced houses destroyed. More attacks followed but East Manchester continued to supply aircraft, fuel additives and munitions for the war effort.

Mayne played their part by transporting military personnel to training camps in Blackpool, with two 1931 AEC Regals (AG 6021 & FV 1786), bought from Lancashire Motors for £475 in July 1940. Bus services were restricted to save fuel, with Mayne's running in the busy peak periods and evenings to enable essential workers to get to and from the factories and collieries. Women were employed as conductors. They used a shaded battery lamp to help them see to collect fares and issue tickets at night. Blackout conditions and the threat of air raids also made driving at night unpleasant and dangerous.

Arthur also served the community as a special constable, based at Mill Street police station in Beswick, along with another Pioneer, James Ferrington. Arthur enjoyed the role and would continue this voluntary work after the war. Like many families, the Maynes also experienced loss too, with Arthur's nephew Peter, mother-in-law Sarah and his wife, Harriett, not living to see the end of the war in 1945.

# POST-WAR CHALLENGES

Fuel restrictions were lifted in December 1945, enabling the off-peak and Sunday bus journeys to be restored, although fuel rationing continued until May 1950. A Bedford OWB bus (GND 994) was utilised on Manor Road until 1949. Some of the damaged Regents also had their bodywork rebuilt by East Lancs, with reconditioned diesel engines fitted. Another pair (TV 4491/945) were obtained from Nottingham, initially pending delivery of new AEC Regent III's (KNA 876/7) in 1949. A labour shortage also led to some of the female conductors being retained, in stark contrast to Manchester's all-male crews.

The trolleybus network had expanded during the war, using Emergency Orders that Manchester Corporation sought to legalise, as well as requesting powers to introduce a route along Manor Road. Mayne's service was suddenly under threat.

Arthur had successfully sued the Corporation in 1943, after discovering the Council's (Business) Rates on Mayne's garage had been inflated. He challenged them again now and the fight went on Appeal all the way to the House of Lords, who ruled that Manchester could not build the trolleybus extension without Mayne's consent.

Perhaps fuelled by the euphoria of his remarkable victory, Arthur asked 21-year-old Olive Brien out to celebrate. The couple got married on 4th July 1946 and, after living in North Wales and then Audenshaw, they eventually settled in Heaton Chapel, near Stockport. Families, re-united for the first time in years, began to pick up the threads of their lives again, as demand for coach travel soared. Revenues rose from £22,598 in 1946 to £39,569 in 1947, as six new AEC Regals and two Bedford OBs increased the coach fleet to 12.

# THE FIFTIES

A dozen AEC Regents were also gradually sourced from the municipal fleets of Leeds, Salford and Glasgow, joining a "utility" Bedford SB (LXJ 318) that cost £2,000 and saw limited use on Manor Road. The Regents are thought to have begun sporting a new maroon and turquoise livery intended to help distinguish them from Manchester's increasingly red buses, see illustrations below. New Ultimate ticket machines also replaced the original Bell Punch models on 14th September 1951.

*Top Row:* JNC 4 was one of four AEC Regal IIIs delivered in 1947/8. Its chassis cost £3,718 and the 33-seat coachwork by Bellhouse Hartwell of Westhoughton a further £1,962 10s. Unlike most early post-war deliveries, they were well-constructed and did not require re-bodying mid-life. It was retired in December 1960. HNE 3/4 originally had 33-seat coachwork by Santus of Wigan before being lengthened and re-bodied by Yeates of Loughborough to this 39-seat design in January 1954, enabling them to serve another nine seasons with Mayne/Dean. *(RM)*

*Above left:* Two 1935 AEC Regents (AUM 407/434) that had been re-bodied by Roe in 1946 were acquired from Leeds Corporation in October 1950 and operated until 1963/4. AUM 407 is seen on Manor Road near Edge Lane, preparing to return to the Sunnyside estate, where it would terminate near Springfield Road. *(BL)*

*Above right:* Two 8.8-litre Regents were acquired from Salford City Transport. RJ 8726 arrived in 1950 for spares and was followed in 1951 by RJ 8728 which managed a further ten years' service with Mayne. It initially had three stripes, similar to the Salford livery, before gaining a simplified destination display, green light and lettering advertising the private hire operation. Note the conductor with an Ultimate ticket machine. *(BL)*

*Upper left:* After trialling three petrol-powered Bedford SBs in 1951/2, two further batches were purchased in 1955/6. All but the Mulliner bus (LXJ 318) were fitted with Duple's 41-seat Vega coachwork. SVM 4 entered service in April 1956 and is seen here in Southport in 1960. They were replaced by diesel-powered Bedfords in 1963. *(RM)*

*Upper right:* After this 1936 AEC Regent arrived from London Transport in 1952, three more (CXX 377 and DGX 210/2) were acquired in 1953/4 for spares, with DGX 214 eventually meeting the same fate in 1955. *(BL)*

*Above left:* Two 1939 Regents (CUS 812/8) with rear entrance Weymann bodywork were purchased from Glasgow Corporation in January 1953, increasing the bus fleet to twelve. They were joined by CUS 814 in May 1956 and the trio remained in use until 1962/3. *(AC)*

*Above right:* This Bedford SB bus with 34-seat bodywork by Mulliner of Chiswick entered service in July 1951 but saw limited use on Manor Road. It was sold to Harper and Keller of St Agnes, Cornwall in 1955 before passing to McGregor of Ambleside in 1960. His business included a garage, a pub and a bus service to Hawkshead. One of his early customers was Beatrix Potter who may well have immortalised him in *'The Tale of Peter Rabbit'*. *(RD)*

*Right:* The company's first vehicle with Plaxton coachwork was HD 9304, a 1952 AEC Regal IV, seen here in London. It was purchased from Broadhead of Dewsbury in January 1954 and joined by JGE 334, a 1951 example that had 39-seat Yeates coachwork. HD 9304 was sold in December 1959 but JGE 334 lasted until January 1967. *(RM)*

*Left:* An order for four 9.6-litre AEC Regent IIIs was announced in 1947, but only two were delivered in 1949 to replace AXJ 496 and TV 735. KNA 876/7 cost £4,062 each and were fitted with semi-automatic gearboxes, air pressure brakes and rear-entrance East Lancs bodywork. KNA 877 was withdrawn in February 1967. *(AC/FPR)*

The company's general manager, Frank Wade, died suddenly on 8th November at the age of 47. Frank was married to Arthur's sister Olive and had worked for the company for 24 years, becoming a director and shareholder in 1945. It would be three years before Arthur found a suitable replacement. Frank Palmer, a former British Road Services manager, would manage the business for the next 32 years.

The Droylsden excursions licence of Shipleys of Ashton-under-Lyne was acquired on 21st January 1953, enabling Mayne to run day trips from its stage carriage heartland. Larger coaches, such as the AEC Regal IV, were now available with the engine under the floor. Two joined the fleet in 1954, but their heavy fuel consumption led to the Bedford SB becoming increasingly favoured, as it was lighter, cheaper and more economical to run. Eighteen were operated in the 1950s, around half of which were diesel powered.

Arthur, Olive, Matilda, Stephen and Andrew Mayne pictured at Prestatyn in the early 1950s. *(LH)*

Mayne's Garage was extended in 1954, with more of the parking area becoming enclosed and an office built over the motor spares shop. Neon lights were fitted to the frontage to advertise the petrol station, which now accounted for an increasing proportion of the firm's revenue, worth £26,152 in 1953, up from £5,400 in 1946. Total revenue for the year ending November 1953 was £46,434 - around £900,000 in today's money.

This 1953 7.7-litre AEC Regent III was a former demonstrator, fitted with a prototype 58-seat Park Royal body. It was bought from AEC in August 1954 and seen on Dale Street, as a stylish-looking conductor chats to the driver. The bus retained its red, maroon and pale green City of Oxford colours throughout its 18-year stay. *(RM)*

Seen on the forecourt is Regent CVR 1 that was converted into a towing waggon in 1955. Engineer, Tommy Proctor, who spent his working life at Mayne's, is busy moving vehicles to be photographed. *(PM)*

Mayne Garage looking a little tired. The red and turquoise neon lights, fitted around 1954, became as much of a nocturnal trademark as the green lights on the front of the Regents. The petrol pumps are selling fuel from National, a subsidiary of BP and Shell, known originally as National Benzole. Access to the parking area at the rear was initially via the forecourt on the right until the building was extended in the 1980s. *(Mayne)*

An example from the company's Bell Punch bus ticket machines used until 1951. *(AC)*

The Suez crisis led to the re-introduction of fuel rationing for five months from 17th December 1956, affecting their operating costs and ability to sell fuel. Mrs Matilda Mayne, who still played an active role in the business as company secretary, died on 14th February 1957 at the age of 81. Arthur's wife, Olive, was appointed as her successor.

Mayne expanded into North Manchester a month later with the acquisition of F & H Dean Ltd of 26 Old Church Street, Newton Heath. Fred and Harold Dean had started running a hire car and taxi business in the 1920s, entering the day trip market in 1930, after taking on their father's haulage and charabanc work. Their smart green and cream fleet of four Leylands and two Bedfords coaches continued to be run separately to overcome the objections to Mayne's latest expansion. The licence of Barton Tours was also obtained on 18th September, allowing Mayne to run excursions from Mossley Road in Ashton, joining those for Droylsden, Clayton, Beswick, Bradford and West Gorton.

Extra journeys commenced on the Blackpool service at Easter and Whitsuntide in 1958, after booking agents provided evidence of the unmet demand to the Traffic Commissioner. The licence and three coaches of A Lea of Westbourne Road, Denton, were also acquired, taking their catchment area into Audenshaw and Denton from 26th October. Mayne's 17 coaches now consisted of nine Bedford SBs, seven AEC Regals and an AEC Reliance. Dean's ran a trio of Leyland Tigers and three Bedford SBs, bringing the total to 23.

*Above left:* In July 1956 this **AEC Reliance** was acquired from Holts of Oldham and operated until December 1966. It had a synchromesh gearbox, vacuum brakes and Burlingham's popular 41-seat Seagull coachwork. Fleet numbers were introduced in 1959 for the coaches, with the Regal IVs and Reliance allocated 1-3. *(RM)*

*Above right:* Pictured in the Princess Street coach park in Blackpool alongside another of Deans Bedford's - MVR 756 that had Duple Vega coachwork - this 1955 Bedford SB with 36-seat Yeates Riviera III coachwork came from Deans of Newton Heath in March 1957 and operated until May 1961. *(RM)*

The destination display on CUS 812 is set for a short working on service 46 to Edge Lane. The extension of the Manor Road route in January 1958 was a significant milestone; not least for the passengers who no longer needed to change buses at the City boundary. *(GL)*

Three 8ft-wide, 30ft-long Regent Vs entered service in July 1957, fitted with 9.6-litre engines. The 73-seaters were initially restricted to the Audenshaw route, as they were considered difficult to reverse on Sunnyside Road. UNF 11 and 12 were sold to Ward of Epping in June 1974, while UNF 10 soldiered on until June 1976 and was scrapped three months later. (PM & AEC/PRV)

This 1946 Regent II was acquired from Tynemouth in December 1958 and had 56-seat Weymann bodywork. It is seen on a private hire on Victoria Bridge Street, near Salford City Transport's Victoria Bus Station. (PM)

Five diesel-powered Duple Bedford SB1s replaced the Bellhouse Hartwell Regal IIIs in 1959. XNB 13-16 were allocated to Clayton and XNB 17 to Newton Heath. XNB 15 is seen in Blackpool with 2244 NA, one of a pair that replaced the Regal IVs in 1960. They were operated until 1966/7. (PM)

This Duple-bodied Bedford SBG came with the business of Lea of Denton in 1958 along with a Leyland Tiger TS1 (FV 40) and a Seddon (DFV 77). Although the Seddon was repainted red and cream, only the Bedford was operated, taking the coach fleet up to 17, with a further six in the Dean fleet. (RM)

# SERVICE 46

Most passengers using the Manor Road service were heading into Manchester and the transfer at the boundary was becoming increasingly inconvenient. The solution lay in extending the route, so the City's Transport Department were asked if they would agree to run a joint service. They rebuffed the suggestion by applying for their own licence to serve the Sunnyside estate in 1956. Mayne objected and, despite being restricted to operate within Droylsden, sought approval to lodge a counter application to run to Dale Street.

The Traffic Commissioner consented and suggested the two should reach an agreement, but the quarrel continued. A proposal requiring one Mayne Regent was quickly rejected. Undeterred, the company placed an order for three new 30ft-long examples. UNF 10-12 arrived in July 1957, increasing the bus fleet to 15. Their 73-seat Park Royal bodywork made them the largest front-engine buses in the City.

The disagreement was eventually settled when a joint application was made for a core 15-minute service on 4th November. This required two Regents and a Corporation bus, with three more vehicles doubling the frequency at peak times. Manchester would provide these in the summer and Mayne in the winter, utilising their coach drivers. They began co-operating on 25th January 1958, when trolleybus service 215 was halved to every 20 minutes, although a licence was not officially granted until 2nd July.

New service 46 ran limited stop between Stevenson Square and Edge Lane, before observing all stops along Manor Road and Chappell Road to Sunnyside Road, turning via St George's Road and Springfield Road. Fares taken within Droylsden belonged to Mayne, less Manchester's working expenses and vice-versa. The firm now had two routes into the City, with the Audenshaw service still terminating at Dale Street.

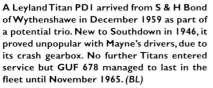

A Leyland Titan PD1 arrived from S & H Bond of Wythenshawe in December 1959 as part of a potential trio. New to Southdown in 1946, it proved unpopular with Mayne's drivers, due to its crash gearbox. No further Titans entered service but GUF 678 managed to last in the fleet until November 1965. *(BL)*

# CHAPTER 4: STAYING INDEPENDENT

**E**ast Manchester began to experience significant decline as British manufacturing lost its competitive advantage to overseas markets. Its textile mills and engineering works began to close, along with its colliery, with the eventual loss of over 35,000 jobs.

As its population moved away in search of work, the Council started demolishing Beswick's old housing in 1967 to build a series of tower blocks that would be poorly assembled and last barely 20 years. The last of the family's shops on Ashton New Road also closed, as the houses, shops, pubs and community around them gradually disappeared.

Mayne started to change their catchment area to counter the depopulation. The licence of P & W Prestwich of Higher Openshaw was acquired on 1st May 1964, followed by the business of EN Shipley Ltd of Ashton-under-Lyne on 7th April 1965. Shipley's ran excursions from Ashton and Mossley, along with express services to Blackpool, Rhyl and Scarborough via York. The booking office in Henry Square was retained until 1973/4.

The growth of holiday camps, such as Butlins at Pwllheli and Pontins at Prestatyn, generated additional custom for coach operators. A reduction in special trains to North Wales in 1964, prompted Dean to start an express service to Prestatyn, Rhyl and Pwllheli in 1966. Mayne also acquired licences from Claribel Motors, who were based on Ashton Old Road in Beswick, to run excursions from Stalybridge, Gorton and Ardwick on 12th May 1967.

Fifteen Bedford SB were in operation by 1961, mostly with Duple coachwork. The 1962 order, however, went to Plaxton of Scarborough for its Embassy model, possibly due to Duple introducing its new Bella Vista design. 9086 ND was the second of two Plaxton Bedford SB1s delivered in April that year. *(RM/PM)*

At least one coach was now making a double run to Blackpool each day in the summer, with up to 30 trips running during the illuminations, along with extended tours to the resort at Christmas. Southport and Morecambe also remained popular destinations, despite growing interest in longer journeys following the arrival of the motorway. One popular outing in 1964 was to London Airport to watch the aircraft!

Further inner-city redevelopment led to Dean's closing its doors. Its licences and six Bedfords transferred to Mayne on 17th November 1967, although the trading name lasted until July 1969. Thirteen Bedford SBs were purchased in the 1960s, along with eleven of the larger VAL and VAM models, plus five Bristol LHs. All had diesel engines and Plaxton coachwork, as allegiance switched from Duple to its Scarborough-based rival in 1962.

The last of the original double-deckers (BNF 553) was retired in March 1959 after almost 24 years' service. Despite a solitary Leyland Titan being trialled, Mayne stayed loyal to the Regent, buying three 30ft-long Park Royal examples (6972-4 ND) in 1961. Five more followed in 1964/5, bodied by East Lancs subsidiary Neepsend Coachworks of Sheffield. 8859/60 VR and CXJ 520-2C cost £6,000 each and would be the last, as production of Arthur's favourite bus ceased in 1968, after AEC became part of Leyland.

*Upper left:* The last second-hand Regent came from South Wales in June 1960. It had Weymann bodywork and was operated until November 1965. The houses across the road were demolished in the 1970s as part of Manchester's urban renewal that saw some 200,000 inner city residents relocated. *(PS)*

*Upper right:* Three more Park Royal-bodied Regent Vs (6972-4 ND) were delivered in December 1961, this time with a revised design and a more powerful AV590 engine. *(RM)*

*Lower left:* The early petrol-powered Bedfords were replaced by four diesel SB5 versions in 1963 (2493-6 VM), fitted with 41-seat Plaxton Embassy II coachwork, featuring a revised front dome. *(PM)*

*Lower right:* This 51-seat AEC Reliance with Plaxton's new Panorama coachwork was a 1962 demonstrator acquired in March 1963. It was the first 36ft (11m) coach in the fleet and was soon joined by another (6352 VU) in 1964. *(PM)*

# OPERATING AGREEMENT

Manchester, having tried again to buy Maynes in 1958 and 1961, announced plans in July 1966 to replace its trolleybuses. Mayne's support was crucial if new stage carriage licences were to be granted. An agreement was eventually reached on 7th December that would see them surrender the Audenshaw route in exchange for sole operation of service 46 and 85% of any profits it made. Their original route, having been affected by the closure of Ashton Moss Colliery and increasing car and television ownership, ran for the last time on 31st December. Manchester replaced it with a peak period service 214 from 2nd January, eventually diverting the journeys via North Road in Clayton as part of service 187 (later 217).

Seven of the eleven Regents were necessary to run the bus routes, including one between the Haddon Hall in Droylsden and Audenshaw Grammar School that was licensed from 16th January 1967 until 13th September 1974. Service 46 meanwhile was re-numbered 213 on 2nd January 1968, as part of wider revisions affecting Manchester's Wilmslow Road services.

Two new Regents arrived in January 1964, this time with bodywork by Neepsend of Sheffield. They were operated until July 1980, before being loaned to Stevensons of Uttoxeter who purchased 8860 VR in December. It was sold to Brian Lomas in January 1981 and can usually be found in the Museum of Transport in Manchester. Mayne retained 8859 VR but it was sold and later exported to Kobe, Japan in 2012. (RM)

A final trio of Regent Vs arrived in August 1965, bringing the total to eleven. CXJ 520-2C had Neepsend bodywork and were notorious for their harsh braking due to their powerful airbrakes. CXJ 520C is seen opposite Kershaw Lane in Audenshaw, prior to reversing into North Drive for the return to Manchester. (RM)

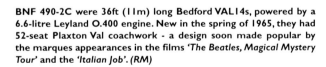

BNF 490-2C were 36ft (11m) long Bedford VAL14s, powered by a 6.6-litre Leyland O.400 engine. New in the spring of 1965, they had 52-seat Plaxton Val coachwork - a design soon made popular by the marques appearances in the films 'The Beatles, Magical Mystery Tour' and the 'Italian Job'. (RM)

This SB5 was delivered in June 1965 with 41-seat Plaxton Panorama coachwork, joining Dean's BBU 958C that had arrived three months earlier with Embassy IV coachwork. The growing popularity of the motor car is evident in this view of Williamson Lane in Droylsden. (RM)

Two more Plaxton Bedford VAL14s (ENE 454/5D) were delivered in April 1966. *(Mayne)*

The weekday timetable for service 213, effective from December 1968.

### SERVICE No. 213.—DROYLSDEN AND STEVENSON SQUARE (Limited Stop)
(Joint service with A. Mayne & Son Limited)

**MONDAY TO FRIDAY**

| | | | | | | | | | | | | | | | |
|---|---|---|---|---|---|---|---|---|---|---|---|---|---|---|---|
| Sunnyside Road | .. | .. | .. | 0540 | 0605 | 0620 | 0635 | 0650 | 0705 | and every | 0935 | and every | 1635 | and every | 1905 |
| Edge Lane | .. | .. | .. | 0546 | 0611 | 0626 | 0641 | 0656 | 0711 | 7¼ mins. | 0941 | 15 mins. | 1641 | 7¼ mins. | 1911 |
| Stevenson Square | .. | .. | .. | 0559 | 0624 | 0639 | 0654 | 0709 | 0724 | to | 0954 | to | 1654 | to | 1924 |
| | | | | | | | | | | | | | | | |
| Sunnyside Road | .. | .. | | and every | 2250 | 2305 | 2320 | | | | | | | | |
| Edge Lane | .. | .. | | 15 mins. | 2256 | 2311 | 2326 | | | | | | | | |
| Stevenson Square | .. | .. | | to | 2309 | .. | .. | | | | | | | | |
| | | | | | | | | | | | | | | | |
| Stevenson Square | .. | | .. | 0600 | 0626 | 0641 | 0656 | 0711 | 0726 | and every | 0911 | and every | 1611 | and every | 1841 |
| Edge Lane | .. | .. | .. | 0613 | 0639 | 0654 | 0709 | 0724 | 0739 | 7¼ mins. | 0924 | 15 mins. | 1624 | 7¼ mins. | 1854 |
| Sunnyside Road | .. | .. | .. | 0619 | 0645 | 0700 | 0715 | 0730 | 0745 | to | 0930 | to | 1630 | to | 1900 |
| | | | | | | | | | | | | | | | |
| Stevenson Square | .. | .. | .. | 1856 | and every | 2226 | 2241 | 2300 | | | | | | | |
| Edge Lane | .. | .. | .. | 1909 | 15 mins. | 2239 | 2254 | 2313 | | | | | | | |
| Sunnyside Road | .. | .. | .. | 1915 | to | 2245 | 2300 | 2319 | | | | | | | |

6974 ND is seen below on Manchester Road heading to Stevenson Square. *(BL)*

31

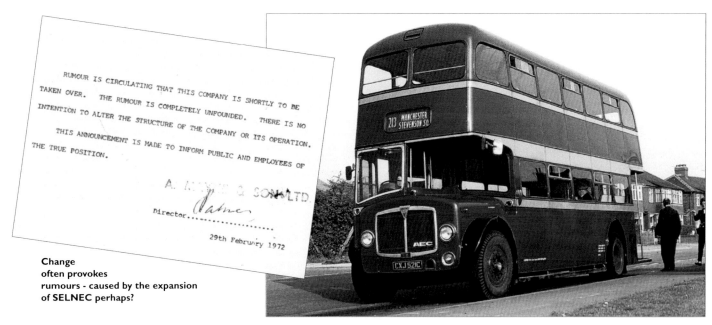

Change
often provokes
rumours - caused by the expansion
of SELNEC perhaps?

CXJ 521C is seen at the Sunnyside Road terminus of the re-numbered 46 - now 213. *(BL)*

Bristol Commercial Vehicles launched its 30ft 'LH' chassis in 1967. TBU 7-9G were delivered in April 1969 and lengthened 36ft LHLs, fitted with Plaxton's new 51-seat Panorama Elite coachwork and a Leyland O.400 engine. They were joined by two LHs with 45-seats in 1970. The LHLs were retired in 1976 and the LHs in 1978. *(PM)*

An eight month old Bedford-powered VAL70 (LVU 885G) was bought from Mayfair of Wythenshawe in November 1969. The acquisition of Connellys of Gorton added another (MVM 824G) in October 1971, just as Mayne's original VAL14s began to be retired. The 52-seaters looked thoroughly modern with their Panorama Elite coachwork, lasting in the fleet until 1977. *(PM)*

The Bedfords were joined by four AEC Reliances (FBU 302-5K) with Plaxton's Panorama Elite Express coachwork. Despite being capable of one-person operation, Mayne usually deployed them on service 213 in peak periods and on Sundays with a two-person crew. The 51-seaters were also used on private hires and excursions (without a conductor!) until 1979/80. *(RM)*

# SELNEC

The Labour Party, led by Harold Wilson, returned to power in 1964 and increased its majority for a second term in 1966. Their ideas for integrating public transport led to the creation of Passenger Transport Executives in the large conurbations, along with the formation of a National Bus Company and Scottish Bus Group.

Implemented under the Transport Act 1968, the South East Lancashire and North East Cheshire PTE was formed on 1st September 1969. Manchester's City Transport department and 10 neighbouring municipal bus undertakings were absorbed on 1st November. The local services of North Western followed in 1972. SELNEC had tried to buy Maynes, but the family decided not to sell. Arthur and Olive had welcomed their eldest son Andrew to the board in 1968. His brother, Stephen, began working in the business in 1971 and their sister, Liz, also later became a shareholder.

A Government grant to encourage the purchase of new vehicles, suitable for one-person operation was doubled to 50% in October 1971, persuading them to begin replacing the venerable AEC Regents. Four AEC Reliance coaches were ordered for contract work and for use on the 213. They entered service in May 1972 in the firm's bus livery, but their narrow aisles were found to be problematic on such a busy route.

Further modernisation came with a £125,000 order for five rear-engine Daimler Fleetlines with Roe bodywork in 1973. Production delays caused by industrial action, a global oil crisis and a three-day working week would delay their arrival until June 1976, by which time they had become a Leyland product.

Local government reform led to Droylsden UDC becoming part of the new Tameside Metropolitan Borough Council in April 1974, when Greater Manchester County Council was also established. SELNEC became Greater Manchester PTE, trading as Greater Manchester Transport and the buses of Wigan Corporation were absorbed. The privately-owned Lancashire United followed in January 1976, leaving just one independent bus operator in Greater Manchester.

The 33ft (10m) long **YRQ** was introduced in 1970 as Bedford's successor to the **VAM**. Mayne took delivery of a pair of 45-seaters in both 1971 (BBU 37/8J) and 1972 (FBU 300/1K), running them until 1978/80. *(PM)*

Four **SB5s** were delivered in 1973, replacing two 1965 examples. LBU 701-4L were 41-seaters and the first Mayne coaches to carry fleet names on their sides. *(Mayne)*

Bedford replaced its **VAL**-chassis in 1972 with the 11m **YRT** but it would be February 1975 before Mayne purchased one. Almost indiscernible in this view of **HBA 696N** in Blackpool, the 53-seater was the first to carry the slogan *'Travel The Mayne Way'* in gold lettering on its sides. *(PM)*

Three more YRTs with Plaxton's timber-framed Panorama Elite coachwork arrived in December. KVU 60-2P were followed by three (11m) turbocharged YMT's and a short wheelbase VAS5 in 1977, fitted with Plaxton's new all steel Supreme coachwork. SBA 200R entered service in June and was operated until 1981. *(PM)*

**Daimler Fleetline LRJ 212P seen in Stevenson Square in 1976.** *(RM)*

Five Gardner-powered Daimler Fleetlines (LRJ 210-4P) (seen on the previous page) replaced the Regents 6972-4 ND and UNF 10 in June 1976. They were followed by a trio of Bristol VRs in 1978 to replace CXJ 520-3C. VJA 666S entered service in April and was followed by VJA 665/7S in June. (PM)

# MAYNE COACHES 1970-9

Although Mayne's bus operation was now unique, many coach firms were still competing in what was now a declining market. They also had to cope with increasing administration, following the introduction of separate UK and European drivers' hours legislation that required Tachograph monitoring devices to be fitted to vehicles by the end of the decade.

The excursions licence and Bedford VAL of Connolly's of Gorton (MVM 824G) were acquired on 22nd October 1971. The firm, based at 261 Hyde Road, had started in the 1930s and had a stake in Star Motors, running works buses to Trafford Park until January 1938.

Another competitor, Morbys, operated from West End Garage, near Edge Lane in Droylsden. They ran excursions from Droylsden and Ashton, having begun with a 32-seat Albion in March 1936, although the origins of the firm were in haulage. Morbys were running two Bedfords and a Leyland Royal Tiger when Mayne bought the business in 1974 and ran it separately until June 1976.

Having bought a Ford Transit from Alf Wilson of Failsworth in December 1974, Mayne returned to buy the Excursions licence and a Ford coach (JCU 800G) on 21st May 1976, although the firm itself continued trading. The business of R Wood & Sons (Tours) Ltd of Ashton-under-Lyne was acquired in July 1979, along with two Bedford SB5s.

Their 23 coaches now consisted of 18 Bedfords (mostly Y-series and SB5s), four AEC Reliances and a Ford Transit. Seven were used on works and council contracts. The company also took supporters to all Manchester City's away games and ran excursions from 16 towns from March until October, including to York and Scarborough on Mondays and Fridays. The holiday services also continued to North Wales and the Fylde coast, with up to ten trips a day to Blackpool, as well as extended tours running there each winter.

This little Bedford VAS5, along with a 12-seat Ford Transit, were the smallest members of the fleet. The 29-seater entered service in July 1977 and was eventually replaced by a Mercedes minibus in August 1981. (PM)

# END OF AN ERA

Although the new double-deckers (LRJ 210-4P) were suitable for one-person operation, Mayne valued the customer service provided by its eleven conductors, some of whom had worked for the company for over 30 years. Around half were women and at least one crew became a married couple. Most were locals and well-regarded.

Rampant inflation and the introduction of the Equal Pay Act increased operating costs by 13% in 1976/7 and profits fell by 9% to £44,078. Unemployment also rose as the power station and more factories and mills closed.

More Fleetlines were needed to reduce costs but Leyland's order book was full, resulting in a switch to the Bristol VRT double-decker. VJA 665-7S re-introduced the red and cream livery to the bus fleet in 1978, as the country and its troubled economy drifted towards its infamous winter of discontent.

The extra Saturday lunchtime journeys on the 213, run originally for mill workers on a five-and-a-half-day week, ceased on 1st April 1979. The Sunday frequency was also halved to every 30 minutes, becoming one person operated. This reduced their scheduled mileage by 8.5% (to 258,962 miles a year), partly in response to another oil crisis.

Tired of it all, Britain elected its first female prime minister and a government intent on privatising public services and promoting free market competition. Mayne, meanwhile, sought to introduce a new route in response to a campaign by local residents to restore connections lost with the closure of Droylsden Station. The 'Lumb Link' service 209 started on 17th December 1979 and followed the route of the 213 to Chappell Road, before continuing to Littlemoss, Lumb Mill. Its hourly frequency was doubled from 10th March 1980, as GMT again sought access to the Sunnyside estate. An agreement was eventually reached on 20th June that permitted GMT's service 346 (later 382) to be extended on 27th July. Plans were also made to introduce the same Almex ticket system as GMT, but the fleet would keep growing and it would be November 1987 before they were finally introduced.

Two more Bristol VRTs (MRJ 8/9W) arrived in July 1980, bringing the AEC Regent's 46-year reign to an end in November - a month that also saw the passing of the company's chairman, Arthur Mayne. His death on 11th November, at the age of 85, dealt a sad blow to the firm in its diamond jubilee year. The loss of a founding generation can lead a company to fall by the wayside, but Stephen Mayne was ready for the challenge, as reforms of the licensing system began to blow more winds of change.

Five YMTs and four SB5s arrived in 1978, receiving S and T registrations, with two YMTs (YNF 348/9T) receiving this attractive new livery. Two more YMTs (HDB 352/3V) followed in 1980, featuring another Plaxton-inspired livery and continuing the series of sequential registrations. *(Mayne)*

# CHAPTER 5:
# DEREGULATION

The Transport Act 1980 abolished the need for licences on long-distance coach routes. This enabled operators to compete and set their own prices on excursions and tours. Mayne's pick-up points grew to include Hyde, Hattersley, Dane Bank and Reddish. They also started replacing the Bedfords with heavier, more powerful Leylands, capable of carrying greater payloads along the growing network of motorways.

Twelve Leyland Leopards and twenty Leyland Tigers were purchased new in the 1980's, including six with a TV/Video, drinks servery and washroom. Along with two Bedford PJKs, the deliveries were shared with a new associate firm, Barry Cooper Coaches of Warrington.

Arnold Barrie Cooper was born in 1936 and grew up on the family's farm in Burtonwood. He opened a grocery shop with his wife Mildred at 1 Mason Street in Howley in 1957. The business prospered and grew to include shops in Wellington Street, Howley and Slater Street, Latchford. Some customers asked if Barry could help them get their children to and from Loreto Convent School in Altrincham, resulting in the purchase of a Commer minibus (636 RTJ) around 1960, that was also used to deliver groceries and for private hire.

Further minibuses and coaches followed, eventually resulting in a move to 110 Grappenhall Road, Stockton Heath in 1969 and the decision to focus on transport. Further premises were also purchased on Sandy Lane from Naylor Motor Services in October 1977.

The first of five Leyland Leopards with Plaxton Supreme IV coachwork is pictured at the 1980 Blackpool coach rally. HDB 354/5V were 11m (53-seat) examples with 6-speed manual gearboxes, while HDB 356/7V were 12m (57-seat) semi-automatics. Last of the batch was MRJ 358W, an 11m (53-seat) semi-auto, fitted with dual purpose coachwork that initially had turquoise stripes instead of maroon. *(Mayne)*

Two more Bristol VRs entered service in July 1980, enabling the last of the Regents to be retired. MRJ 8W is pictured at Manchester University on 12th March 1986. (HSP)

Seven 12m 57-seaters arrived in 1981/2. MRJ 359/60W and SNC 361-5X were joined by a 1970 11m example (WHA 236H) that was rebuilt by Mayne, becoming SNC 366X. Stephen Mayne stands proudly aloft the chassis, prior to its dispatch to Scarborough to receive its new Plaxton Supreme IV coachwork. (Mayne)

As well as school routes, Coopers operated private hires and secured contracts with various Rugby League clubs, including providing transport for the Brazilian football team during the 1966 World Cup. They also developed a speciality for re-building and re-bodying older coaches and equipped the fleet with televisions and CB radios - ideas that Barry adopted from his friend Noel Tatlock, who ran a coach company in Lancashire.

The economic downturn, along with a demand for unpaid tax, led Barry to seek Stephen Mayne's help in 1979. Financial support was provided by a cross company guarantee from 17th December and the business was eventually sold to the Mayne family on 15th January 1982. Re-structured with a £160,000 loan from A Mayne & Son, a new company - Barry Cooper Coaches Ltd - was formed on 14th March with a licence to operate 21 vehicles.

LRJ 210P received commemorative lettering to mark the firm's Diamond Jubilee in 1980. (Mayne)

Leyland Tigers SND 352/3X replaced Bedfords HDB 352/3V in 1982. Intended for new routes, their unusual livery was soon replaced by more traditional versions with 'The MAYNE Group' titles in red (52) and cream (53). They were sold in 1989. (AC)

LRJ 211P was repainted in 1981. The cream section below the lower deck windows was changed to red shortly after. The four other Fleetlines were repainted in 1982/3. (BL)

This 12-seat Mercedes L207D was a Devon Commercial van conversion acquired from O'Brien of Farnworth for a Co-Op works contract in August 1981 and was operated until April 1987. (PH/OS)

Plaxton launched its 3.5m high Paramount 3500 coachwork in 1982 and Mayne purchased two examples in March 1983. ANA 367/8Y were 53-seat Express versions, with two-piece in-swing doors and destination equipment. The coaches started to receive dateless registrations from November 1985, with number 67 becoming OJT 923 in March 1986. Seen here at Wembley, it served in the fleet until February 1993. (PM)

# CUTTING FARES AND COSTS

Mayne wanted to extend service 209 to the Hartshead estate in Ashton, following requests from residents for a service to Manchester. GMT objected but the Traffic Commissioner approved the extension from 8th December 1980, increasing their annual mileage to 302,544, requiring nine vehicles.

Having introduced several fare increases on behalf of GMT in the 1970s, Mayne suggested reducing fares to encourage travel. The 'Great Spring Fare Saving' experiment began at Easter in 1981 and generated a 10% increase in patronage. This was not enough to cover the 38% reduction in fares, however, and the promotion ceased nine months later.

One-person operation was fully adopted on Tuesday 26th May 1981 when a common route was introduced, via Sunnyside Road and Greenside Lane towards Manchester, enabling the frequency of the 213 to be halved. This reduced costs by 7p a mile and, along with the end of the fares experiment, increased profits by 60% to £114,154 on revenues of £375,335 in 1981/2, despite the country entering recession. Mayne also began serving Ancoats Hospital instead of Pollard Street and evening journeys were introduced to Hartshead.

GMT thwarted Mayne's next idea by introducing their own service 189 to link the Beswick and Clayton estates with Manchester and Droylsden in 1984. A more speculative proposal to run a two-hourly express service between Manchester and Barnsley (via Openshaw, Ashton, Stalybridge and Holmfirth) also received a less than enthusiastic response.

Three former London Fleetlines increased the bus fleet to 13 by 1985, reducing their dependency on coaches for support, as two-way radios were fitted to the fleet and a vehicle numbering system was reintroduced. The petrol forecourt also became self-service and the car spares shop was converted into a convenience store to further increase revenue.

Two executive specification versions (A369/70 HNC) joined the Manchester fleet in 1983/4. The Hydracyclic gearbox fitted to number 69 resulted in poor fuel consumption, however, leading to its early disposal, not long after it had received the dateless registration SXU 708 in 1986. *(HSP)*

Mayne buses 1976-1986. UNF 10 is seen at Mayne Garage in early 1976, while some of its replacements sit in the same spot in 1984, ready for peak workings on service 209. *(BL)*

London Transport Fleetline, OJD 163R arrived from Stevensons of Uttoxeter in November 1982, and is seen operating a shuttle service for the Co-Op's Shopping Giant store in Failsworth. VJA 667S was the first of the Bristol VR's to be repainted for their new services in Glossop in March 1986 and is seen below in Stevenson Square shortly after. *(BL/PH)*

# ALL CHANGE

The Government, anxious to cut public transport subsidies, announced that it would deregulate bus services and open them up to competition from 26th October 1986. Greater Manchester PTE would then have to subsidise essential yet unprofitable journeys through competitive tender. Its bus operations would also be separated into a limited company, known as GM Buses, paving the way for its eventual privatisation. This was expected to lead to better services, lower fares and fewer subsidies.

Mayne, already accustomed to operating on a commercial footing, decided to trial several new routes before deregulation, utilising relaxations in the licensing rules. Two off-peak services began on 14th April between Glossop and Manchester (Piccadilly) via the M67 and Hyde Road that were marketed as 'High Peak Pacers'. Service 228 served Hadfield, Tintwistle and Hollingworth, while the 229 served Simmondley and Broadbottom. A shopper's service 238 also started between Ashton and Simmondley, every two hours via Stalybridge and Mottram, with one vehicle on each route. The services were intended to compete with the railway service from Glossop to Manchester which was severely overcrowded at rush hour. Despite the comfortable, refurbished coach-seated double-deckers it was not a success.

The 209 and 213 would be replaced too, taking their buses further into Tameside and out to Oldham from 16th June. New services 232-4 ran every hour from Piccadilly to Hartshead and Oldham (232); Smallshaw and Hazelhurst (233); and Tameside Hospital, Mossley and Micklehurst (234), requiring six buses. An express service 231 to Sunnyside Road doubled the frequency to every 10 minutes at peak times using the buses from the Glossop routes.

In the evenings and on Sundays there were alternate departures on the 231/2, along with Sunday journeys to Hazelhurst (233) and Uppermill (235) that ceased at deregulation.

The excursions programme meanwhile gained pick-up points in Glossop, Middleton and Piccadilly. Holiday express services were also trialled to Morecambe, Pwllheli and Skegness, along with short tours to France, Holland and Ireland. Their new general manager, Peter Townley, who had joined them from Cumberland Motor Services, also developed plans for express coach services to Blackburn, Liverpool and London. Mr Townley was no stranger to the Manchester area having begun his career as a BET trainee with the North Western Road Car Company. He joined Mayne following the break up of the National Bus Company.

This Bedford PJK, fitted with 29-seat Plaxton Supreme IV coachwork, entered service in April 1984. A sister vehicle, A421 KBA, was operated by Barry Cooper. Bedford stopped producing commercial vehicles in 1987 and both PJKs were sold in November 1990, ending 45 years of Bedford operation. *(Mayne)*

Only six Gardner-powered Leyland Tigers were built with manual gearboxes and The Mayne Group had five, including the only two Paramount 3200II versions. B349/50 RNA entered service in May 1985, later becoming LIB 6439 and 403 BGO. *(HW)*

Two more London DMS Fleetlines were purchased from Stevensons in January 1985. OJD 131R arrived in this Stevenson-style livery and was allocated the fleet number 1 later that year. After receiving the standard livery in 1990, it was transferred to Warrington in January 1994 and withdrawn in October 1998 for parts. *(Mayne/GMTS)*

Post London, OUC 35R was operated by Sewards of Dalwood from July 1984 before passing to Happy Days of Woodseaves in October who had its green stripes painted black. It was loaned by Mayne to Barry Cooper until March 1985 who repainted the middle panels red. Seen here on Manor Road, number 5 would eventually gain the standard livery in 1988 and was withdrawn for spares in March 1995. *(BL)*

The 1978 Bristol VRs would be repainted into a new livery for the High Peak Pacers, with number 17 being the first in March 1986. It is seen here on the M67 at Denton on the first day of service 228 on 14th April, operating the 1120 departure from Glossop. *(HSP)*

# EXPANSION

Three more buses were needed from 26th October to run new services 171/2 (Belle Vue - Newton Heath/Higginshaw) and 175 (Higginshaw - Oldham - Woodhouses), mostly along roads no longer served by GM Buses. Service 234 was also extended to the Carrbrook estate, near Stalybridge, increasing Mayne's annual mileage to around 750,000, with 99% of it running without public subsidy.

Not all the ideas worked. The services to Glossop ceased on 14th March 1987, followed by the 171/5 on 12th April. Service 172 was briefly extended from Belle Vue to Stockport and the 231-4 increased to every 15 minutes to relieve overcrowding. The 231 became a regular stopping service, initially to Waterloo in Ashton, and then Smallshaw from 5th July.

Deregulation had encouraged local coach firms, as well as neighbouring municipal and National Bus Company concerns to run buses in Greater Manchester, increasing the number of operators to 41. A minibus operation called Bee Line started in January 1987, prompting GM Buses to develop its own network to see off the threat. Timetables and routes now changed frequently, as operators developed their services and competed with one another.

GMPTE tried to fill significant gaps in the network by subsidising replacement journeys, providing welcome extra work for companies like Mayne. Some of their first contracts took them into Stockport, with Sunday journeys on service 22 (to

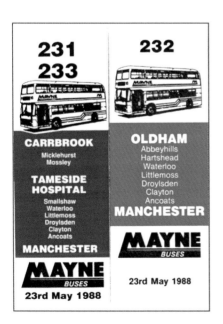

Eccles and Swinton) and 394 (Hazel Grove – Lane Ends) from 12th April. They also operated services 291-4 (Streford – Trafford Park) for five months from the 23rd May.

Their long association with the summer Sunday and Bank Holiday service 395 (Manchester - Castleton via Glossop) began on 3rd May 1987, under contract to Derbyshire County Council. It would be joined by the 396 via Stockport in 1988 and the Pennine Rambler 460 (Rochdale - Matlock Bath) in 1989. Mayne also replaced GM Buses Sunday journeys on the 216 and 236 along Ashton New Road from 21st June 1987.

This 1973 Leyland Leopard, seen in 1995, originally had Van Hool Vistadome coachwork and the registration ORO 325L. Owned by Barry Cooper from July 1985 to September 1986, it was fitted with a 218bhp Leyland TL11 engine and rebodied by Duple before entering service with Mayne as ASV 764. It moved back to Warrington in January 2000 and was up seated to 70 before being sold in January 2003. *(MH)*

Three executive Tigers with Gardner engines were delivered in 1987. C347/8 YBA joined the Mayne fleet, while C426 YBA entered service with Barry Cooper. C347YBA became LIB 6437 in October 1988 and converted to a standard 53-seat layout in October 1997. It was destroyed in an arson attack at the Fairclough Street yard in November 2002 along with 403 BGO (B350 RNA) and P75 JND. *(HW)*

Nine Leyland Leopard buses were bought from West Yorkshire PTE in March 1987, with four for Barry Cooper. UJX 916M was new to Halifax Corporation in 1973 as its number six and wore the same number with Mayne. GWY 691N was intended for Barry Cooper but exchanged for SCP 342L in October. The 'Yorkshire Puddings' were replaced by newer examples from Merthyr Tydfil in November 1988, with Barry Cooper continuing to run them on Cheshire Bus contracts until 1990. *(BL)*

| 4 | 172 |
|---|---|
| ASHTON<br>Stalybridge<br>Millbrook<br>Carrbrook<br>Micklehurst<br>MOSSLEY<br>Tameside<br>Hospital | HIGGINSHAW<br>OLDHAM |
| **MAYNE** *BUSES* | **MAYNE** *BUSES* |
| 23rd May 1988 | 18th January 1988 |

# IMPROVING THE FLEET

Chief Engineer, Gradyn Thompson, who had joined them from Finglands in 1983, became general manager in February 1988 following the departure of Mr Townley to take charge of transport in Lincoln. He continued improving the fleet, with smartly presented former GMT, West Yorkshire and Merthyr Tydfil buses. Mayne now had 18 buses, 20 coaches and employed 50 people, with a further 20 vehicles and 30 staff at Barry Cooper Coaches.

The 172 was curtailed to run between Higginshaw and Oldham on 18th January 1988 and would last another eighteen months. GMPTE sought a replacement for the section between Newton Heath and Chorlton but Mayne failed to win the contract.

The resources were used instead to launch service 424, introducing new links between Ashton and the Fitton Hill estate in Oldham. The two buses on the 20-minute service worked independently until service 4 started between Ashton, Stalybridge and Carrbrook on 23rd May. This enabled them to be linked up with a revised 233 at Carrbrook, allowing driver changeovers to take place in Clayton. GM Buses launched competing journeys on 15th August but soon retreated, having underestimated the loyalty of Mayne's customers.

More GMPTE contracts were won, taking them to the north and west of the conurbation on service 55 (Eccles – Pendleton) from 15th August, service 500 (Bolton - Manchester Airport) from 25th September and service 139 (Manchester – Prestwich) from 3rd April 1989, as the first of five new Scania double-deckers entered service. GM Buses service 357 (Ashton – Audenshaw – Littlemoss) was also replaced without subsidy from 2nd May.

The contract to run the hospital visitors service 177 (Belle Vue – North Manchester General) started on 26th August, along with Sunday journeys on the 196/7 (to East Didsbury) a month later. There were also works services to Trafford Park and eight school routes, including one in Wigan that was subcontracted to Barry Cooper. The Mayne fleet was now operating more efficiently and had a presence in all ten districts of Greater Manchester. It was quite an achievement, but more was to come in the decade ahead, as competition between the different companies intensified.

Some 600 GMT buses were withdrawn at deregulation. 15 Gardner-powered Fleetlines, mostly with Northern Counties bodywork, were bought between 1987 and 1989, including five for parts. The first is seen here prior to entering service in July 1987. Number 18 was operated until September 1993. *(BL)*

A sight Arthur could only dream of - a Manchester bus in Mayne's colours operating the former tram route along Ashton New Road. Number 4 was one of six that entered service in 1988, later operating in Warrington from 1994 until circa 2002. This part of Piccadilly would be closed from 24th September 1989 for construction of a new Metrolink tram platform, with Mayne moving their services to the Arndale Bus Station. (DF)

Mayne's last GMT Fleetline arrived in August 1989 and retained the livery of its previous operator Hulme Hall Coaches. Originally XJA 566L, it had the dateless registration CSU 918 until September 1991, when it became DRJ 917L. It was the third GMT standard to be withdrawn in 1991, with the last leaving in 1994. (BL)

This Atkinson Borderer was new in 1974 to a Birmingham haulier as POG 182M. Converted to a recovery truck, it is pictured rescuing LRJ 211P in 1986, close to where the Mayne's furniture shops once were. (BL)

Two Cummins-powered Tigers with Duple coachwork were delivered in January 1989, some six months before rival Plaxton bought Duple's production rights. F55 HNC was an executive 53-seat Duple 340, while number 56, was a standard 57-seat Duple 320 with an automatic gearbox. They were sold in April 1996. *(HW)*

Three Willowbrook-bodied Leyland Leopard buses (NTX 361-3R) were bought from Merthyr Tydfil at the end of 1988, becoming numbers 23-5, with a fourth (NTX 360R) acquired for parts in May 1990. Number 23 is seen in Ashton Bus Station on service 357 on 11th May 1987, accompanied by Bee Line minibuses. *(HW)*

This Duple Dominant-bodied Leopard was purchased from Merthyr Tydfil in November 1989. Initially number 69, it was re-numbered 24 in March 1991 after two of the older Welsh Leopards were sold. It is seen in Eccles on service 55 to Pendleton, a subsidised route whose popularity grew under Mayne's stewardship. *(BL)*

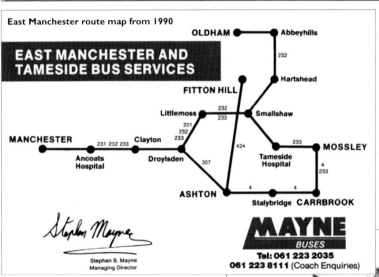

East Manchester route map from 1990

**EAST MANCHESTER AND TAMESIDE BUS SERVICES**

Stephen B. Mayne
Managing Director

**MAYNE** BUSES
Tel: 061 223 2035
061 223 8111 (Coach Enquiries)

Their first new buses since 1980 were two Scania N113 with Northern Counties 'Palatine' bodywork. F112 HNC arrived in March 1989, followed by F113 HNC in May, when this picture was taken. Renowned for their speed and comfort, they would become their longest-serving rear engine buses. Three more (G115-7 SBA) would be delivered during the winter of 1989/90, the last of which carried commemorative lettering to mark the company's '70 Years of Friendly Service'. *(BL/HW)*

When Regent V 8860 VR was withdrawn at the end of 1980 it was purchased for preservation, and is seen here at a rally in Halifax some 14 years later, looking pristine and providing a reminder of how smart Mayne's buses were kept. *(JAS)*

213X DROYLSDEN SUNNYSIDE RD

8860 VR

# CHAPTER 6: COMPETITION

The Mayne way of running reliable services with smartly presented vehicles and drivers was soon helping turn some subsidised routes, such as the 55 and 139, into profitable commercial ventures. Service 55 was extended from Pendleton to Manchester (Arndale) and the 139 from Prestwich to Bury from 11th November 1990.

There were extensions to the core network too with services 4 and 357 becoming new services 234/5 between Manchester, Stalybridge and Carrbrook, with the 235 initially running via Audenshaw. The 424 was also extended from Fitton Hill to Oldham, as the first of three Leyland Leopards were fitted with Willowbrook's new Warrior bus body to modernise their appearance.

Although the 25 buses were operating more efficiently, the 21 coaches remained the backbone of the business providing private hire, excursions and holiday express services. With space in Mayne Garage at a premium, the coaches moved to Fairclough Street in Clayton in the summer of 1989. Built alongside the railway arches that once carried coal trains into the power station, the former haulier's yard was originally a tarpaulin works and increased the Mayne Group premises to four.

A series of UK and European coach holidays began in 1990, using two DAF-powered Bova Futura's (G57/8 SBA). This increased in 1991 to include pick-up points in Altrincham, Sale, Stretford, Pendleton, Eccles, Swinton, Pendlebury, Rochdale, Oldham and Warrington. Two new Dennis Javelins, fitted with Duple coachwork, also joined the fleet. The tours proved popular, especially those to Ireland, Scotland and the new Euro-Disney theme park, as did the air-holidays to Jersey, leading to more departure dates in 1992.

Two Dutch-built Bova Futuras entered service in February 1990. Number 58 is seen in Ashton on 17th March, promoting UK and European holidays. Sister vehicle, number 57, was painted cream with red stripes. Both stayed in the fleet until the end of 1998. *(HW)*

MRJ 358W became MJI 5766 and number 66 in February 1990 before also gaining red stripes. It is seen in Manchester's Albert Square on 11th November, operating the experimental 174/5 circulars that were run for GMPTE along with a six-month contract for service 74 (Manchester–Pendleton) from 20th May 1990. *(HW)*

The last of their Roe-bodied Fleetlines received a repaint in 1989 and soldiered on until November 1990. *(BL)*

The three DMSs and two 1980 VRs were also repainted, with number 3 receiving this interim all-over advert for the Every Bus Saver ticket. It is seen at the Trans Lancs Rally at Heaton Park in September 1990. *(BL)*

# FLEETLINES AND FALCONS

Six former GM Buses staff established Pennine Blue and started competing with their old employer and Mayne in Mossley in March 1990. They began serving Droylsden in April 1991 when service 381 (Ashton - Hazelhurst) was extended to Sunnyside Road. This prompted GM Buses to increase its 382 and extend it along Manor Road to Manchester on 21st April.

Under attack again, Mayne withdrew service 55 on 7th May and extended the popular 424 to Manchester (Stevenson Square), providing new links along Ashton Road West and Props Hall Drive in Failsworth. A direct route to Bury was also introduced. Service 140 avoided the traditional detour around Carr Clough, offering a reliable alternative to the train service that was about to undergo conversion to Metrolink.

They provided rail replacement services too, while the lines from Bury to Manchester and Altrincham were converted from 5th August 1991 until 12th June 1992. Four peak journeys were retained on service 9 (Altrincham - Manchester) until 14th August in a short-lived attempt to compete with the new trams.

To keep up with the changes, several London B20 Fleetlines entered service, alongside six Dennis Falcon single-deckers from Oxford and Chesterfield, increasing the bus fleet to 36. Electronic ticket machines were also introduced in July and the company would try to buy Shearings bus services in Bolton when they were offered for sale at the end of the year.

GM Buses made further cuts to its network on 6th April 1992, tempting Pennine Blue to divert its 381 away from Droylsden. Mayne replaced GM's services 329 and 332 (Ashton - Hurst Cross/Hartshead) utilising resources released from the Bury rail replacements. Having been denied the chance to retain the routes with public subsidy, GM Buses retaliated with competing journeys on the 140 and 424 from 12th April and extended services 168/9 to Tameside Hospital via the Sunnyside estate. The 382, now running solely between Littlemoss and Manchester, would be re-numbered 231 on 7th September.

This 1980 Alexander-bodied Seddon Pennine IV was new to Eastern Scottish and acquired from Stevensons in January 1991. Seen here in Fitton Hill, it was sold to Pioneer Travel of Rochdale in August 1993. (BL)

The chassis of Leopards NRE 382L and RBF 987M were bought in May 1990, becoming LIW 1322/3 after receiving new Willowbrook bodywork in December, along with NIB 7625 (NTX 362R). The 48-seaters were withdrawn in 1995/6, with 23 loaned to Barry Cooper in 1997. 25 is pictured on Crabtree Lane, ready for an evening contract on service 188 that Mayne ran for just over two years from 25th March 1991. (BL)

This unique Dennis Falcon came in part-exchange for MRJ 8/9W in January 1991 and is seen here in Droylsden being shadowed by a GM Buses Leyland Atlantean. A101 DPB was new to Alder Valley in 1983 and re-bodied after a fire in 1987 with similar Wadham Stringer bodywork. The bus was soon painted into fleet livery and its destination display was replaced with a conventional one in April 1996 following electrical problems. Having spent much of 2000 in storage, number 21 moved to Warrington in July 2001 and was withdrawn after an accident in March 2004. (BL)

The extra competition spelt the end for Mayne's commercial operation along Bury New Road. Service 140 was withdrawn on 5th October 1992, when the 139 was curtailed to run between Manchester and Prestwich again. Most journeys ceased three months later, with the remainder eventually becoming part of the subsidised service 96 to Simister.

In Tameside, service 329 was absorbed into the 232-5, that now all ran via Littlemoss and as circular routes between Ashton and Mossley from 5th October 1992. The Audenshaw section of the 235 was briefly replaced by new service 186 (to Tameside Hospital) and the 332 was extended to from Hartshead to Oldham, Hollinwood and Manchester. The two would merge six months later to form another large circular, numbered 332/6.

*Below left:* Special B20 versions of the Fleetline entered service in London in 1977, with a turbocharged Leyland O.690 engine. Eight were purchased in March 1991 with parts from **THX 496S** used to replace the centre doors and increase their capacity from 68 to 75 seats. Their destination displays were also replaced with parts from **GMT** Fleetlines. Number 31 was the third into service in August and is seen waiting at Tameside Hospital. *(MH)*

*Above right:* Five more B20s followed in 1992/4 but only **THX 619S** entered service. Number 19 is seen in Piccadilly with number 35 (**THX 555S**) in June 1996. The latter would be withdrawn following an accident two months later. The remaining B20s were replaced in 1997/8, with four seeing further service in Warrington until 2002. *(MH)*

*Right:* The B20 version of the Fleetline was immediately recognisable from the rear with its noise-reducing cowls.

*Below left:* Two Dennis Javelins arrived in the spring of 1991 from a batch of stock vehicles produced by Duple before its closure. Number 51 was an 8.5m Duple 320 fitted with 37 seats which replaced the Bedford PJK in March. Re-registered SIW 6251 in August 1996, it was later repainted cream. Sister vehicle 52 (H52 FDB), was an 11m, 57-seater (later 55). Both were operated until September 1998. *(HW)*

*Below right:* This ERF B-series vehicle was originally a tractor unit for towing articulated trailers but converted by **PVS** of Barnsley into a recovery truck in 1991. It passed into Stagecoach ownership in 2008 but was soon sold. *(Mayne/AC)*

This Leyland-powered Tiger was new to Kelvin Scottish in April 1987 as D323 RNS and had 46-seat Duple 340 coachwork for use on Scottish Citylink routes from Glasgow. It later passed to Highland Scottish and was bought by Mayne in September 1991. Re-registered three months later, it was operated until September 1994. *(PM)*

Number 65 (formerly SNC 365X) is seen on Chatham Street in Manchester on 11th February 1992 operating the weekday rail replacement service 9 to Altrincham via Timperley. Mayne would retain four journeys in a brief attempt to compete with the new trams later that summer. *(HW)*

Five Dennis Falcons were purchased from Chesterfield Transport in November 1991. A44-8 YWJ were the only Marshall-Camair bodied versions built. Number 46 is pictured in Ashton on service 341 that was run under an emergency contract during the summer of 1992. The 53-seaters were replaced by new Dennis Darts in 1997/8 after consideration was given to buying two East Lancs Falcons from Hyndburn. *(HW)*

Three Gardner-powered Fleetlines (GSC 857T & ULS 663/6T) from the Clydeside fleet of Western Scottish increased the bus fleet to 40 in November 1992. ULS 663T had an automatic transmission and is pictured in Lever Street bus station on the 28th June 1993. Withdrawn in August 1995, it joined number 6 at Warrington in April 1996, where they were used on school contracts until July 2000. (HW)

After running GMPTE school contracts in south Manchester, Mayne gained work closer to home and was operating 18 school runs in Manchester and Tameside by 1993. Here, a trio of buses are on Manor Road on services 731/2 to Littlemoss and Ashton in 1995. (JAS)

# DARTS AND DOMINATORS

Having strengthened their presence in Oldham, an initial five-year contract was won to run services 171/2 (Newton Heath – Withington Hospital) from 9th November 1992, enabling the first of four new Dennis Darts to be purchased.

Mayne added another corridor to its network when it replaced the Ashton Old Road service 220 to Stalybridge on 11th January 1993. The evening and Sunday journeys, along with those on the 169 (Droylsden – Southern Cemetery) followed on 28th February. A new subsidised service 170 (Haughton Green – Withington Hospital) also replaced service 349 that Mayne had been running to Ryder Brow since 25th November 1991 and it would gradually be extended to Cheadle and Adswood.

Plans were made to trial a Dennis Dominator double-decker alongside another Scania with Northern Counties bodywork, but three Dominators were subsequently obtained from a cancelled order at East Lancs, entering service in March 1993. The Scania (L114 DNA) followed in August after receiving similar bodywork, increasing the fleet to 64 (44 of them buses), with Barry Cooper operating a further 23.

The circular 332/6 were replaced by a simplified service 434 (Ashton – Hollinwood – Manchester) on 31st January 1994, freeing up resources to run the subsidised services 290-2 to Trafford Park again. 33 buses were now necessary to run the daytime network.

GM Buses, having been split into two (North and South) by the Government, ready for privatisation, was by now battling with newcomer MTL Manchester, who were operating around 150 buses from a base in Miles Platting. Mayne were soon caught in the crossfire, leading to the withdrawal of the 424 and 434 on 30th August 1994, as the number of operators topped other UK cities at 61.

**18th April 1993**

MANCHESTER - ASHTON

**NEW** 332 336 424 **REVISED**

A. MAYNE & SON LTD.
Ashton New Road,
Clayton,
Manchester,
M11 4PD.
TEL: 061-223 2035

MAYNE BUSES

East Lancs Dennis Dominator's K36/7 YNE & K38 YVM entered service in March 1993. Number 38 is pictured with one of two new Dennis Darts delivered a few months earlier. Despite their Gardner engines, the Dominators were slower and less reliable than the Scanias and were sold to London & Country in January 1996. *(DB)*

Two more 9.8m Dennis Darts (L26/7 FNE) arrived in 1994, as GM South doubled its 231 to every 10 minutes or less. Number 26 is seen on Sunnyside Road with a Dennis Falcon, after Mayne increased its combined frequencies to every 5-7 minutes. *(JAS)*

Twenty-four Trent Barton Leopards were purchased in a deal with PVS of Barnsley in August 1994, with seven passing to The Mayne Group. KVO 144/5W came to Manchester and became regulars on the 290/1, receiving dateless registrations in June 1996. They were withdrawn in April 1997. Siblings KVO 142/6W were considered for fitment with East Lancs EL2000 bodywork, but new single-deck buses were purchased instead. *(MH)*

Two Northern Counties Scania L113 arrived in November and December 1994. M42 ONF was a 51-seater, while M113 RNK was a former demonstration vehicle with 49 seats. Number 42 is seen in Dukinfield. *(HW)*

Two double-deck Scanias with East Lancs bodywork followed in February 1995, increasing the type to ten. The second of the batch was painted in the old bus livery to mark the firm's 75th anniversary. *(BL)*

Various low-floor Scania L113 models were trialled on new service 167 in 1995. This example, seen here at Market Street in Droylsden on 27th July, had bodywork by Wrights of Ballymena. Mayne would eventually purchase the bus a decade later from Stephensons of Essex. *(HW)*

Falcon number 48 is seen on Portland Street, Manchester, on service 290 to Trafford Park. (JAS)

New to the Royal Arsenal Co-Operative Society as JVS 928N, this 1975 Leopard was originally fitted with a Duple Dominant coach body. Perry of Bromyard sent it to receive a new Willowbrook Warrior bus body in December 1989 and sold it to Mayne in February 1990. The 51-seater moved to Warrington in September 1999 but was soon sold to Silver Star of Caernarfon. It was later exported to Ireland as 90-G-1849. (JAS)

Even the King has travelled The Mayne Way! The then HRH Prince of Wales seen on a tour of the region in the 1990s with C347 YBA. (Mayne)

An existing order for a new Scania was deferred until August 1993, so K114 XNE became L114 DNA and received East Lancs bodywork instead of the originally intended Northern Counties design. (BL)

# BATTLE OF THE BUSES

As new housing estates were built in Littlemoss, GM South gradually increased its 231 to every 10 minutes. Mayne responded by increasing its peak frequency and introducing a new service 167 (Droylsden - Littlemoss - Ashton) on 28th August 1994 to defend its core network. Four new Scanias also arrived, increasing the type to 10.

Pennine Blue, having been unable to replace its elderly fleet, was sold to Potteries Motor Traction of Stoke in November 1993. They invested in new Dennis Darts and began to mirror the 232-5 around Mossley from 29th August 1994, as new Sunday trading laws increased patronage and traffic on what was traditionally the quietest day of the week. Ashton New Road competitor, Dennis's, also expanded onto Ashton Old Road on 1st September, quickly turning it into another hotbed of competition.

GM South, now employee-owned, doubled services 168/9 to every 10 minutes on 18th September and reduced its fares to 99p. Residents in Droylsden were less than impressed with the increase in buses (to 26 an hour) though and Tameside Council threatened to introduce traffic-calming measures. It also announced plans to develop Droylsden and Ashton Moss with an extension of Metrolink and the M60 motorway.

Mayne weathered the storm until GM South finally capitulated on 2nd September 1995, when their 231, Mayne's 167 and their 4½-year battle ceased. Just when it seemed things might return to normal, Manchester City Council closed Market Street to buses, forcing the 231-5 to terminate near Piccadilly Gardens when work finished on 3rd December.

Pennine Blue assembled an often smart but elderly fleet. This Park Royal-Leyland Atlantean was new to Southdown in 1974 before passing to Ribble. It is seen here in Ashton Bus Station on service 381 on 7th September 1991. *(HW)*

Indirect competition came from Bee Line and C-Line between 1990 and 1996. This former Crosville Leyland National is seen on Lever Street on 13th September 1991. (HW)

One of eight Mercedes 709D bought by Dennis's in 1994. Dennis McCarthy diversified from taxi and chauffeur-driven hire cars to operating coaches in 1968. The business passed to daughter Marjorie and son-in-law Roy Cooper, who began running bus services in 1986. They began a fast service to Manchester, just like Arthur Mayne did. Their success on the 216 led to them running along the 219 route from 1994. (JAS)

Dennis's low-floor Dart P547 HVM is pictured with Mayne's Scania number 10, GM South's MCW Metrobus 5180, and Leyland Olympian 3010 in Magic Bus livery. The Magic Bus low-fare operation began in 1996 along Wilmslow Road and Stockport Road, later appearing on the Ashton Old and New Roads too. (JAS)

In addition to the former **GM Buses** repainted into Magic Bus livery **Stagecoach** also purchased several Dennis Dragons which had previously been new to Stagecoach Kenya in 1996 and imported back to the UK in 1998. Their high capacity made them ideal for the Wilmslow Road corridor. They would also later be used on the Ashton corridors. *(JAS)*

Cascaded from the city Centreline routes onto service 168 between Longsight and Tameside Hospital, this 24-seat Dennis Domino made an unusual appearance on the 216 on 11th March 1994. *(HW)*

Potteries Motor Traction bought **Pennine Blue** in 1993 and purchased eight Marshall-bodied Darts in 1994. These were later joined by Plaxton examples from the parent fleet, like L940 LRF seen here in Ashton. **PMT** became part of First Group in April 1995. *(HW)*

M210 NDB basks in the sun in Manchester's Piccadilly in 1996. Behind, GM South's 5180 is operating service 236, the former North Western service 6 along Ashton New Road to Glossop. *(JAS)*

Two 12m Dennis Javelins with 55-seat UVG Unistar coachwork arrived in February and March 1996. N67/8 YVR were pre-production models, based on Wadham Stringer's Vanguard II design, built for the Ministry of Defence. They would serve Mayne for over 20 years, being up-seated to 69 and re-registered BIG 4667/8 in March 2006. Number 67 is seen in the Fairclough Street yard in July 1996. (MH)

Like the Javelins, this Bova Futura Club was powered by a Cummins engine. Entering service in May 1996, the 55-seater was re-registered SIL 3856 in March 2000 and operated until August 2011. (MH)

Fleetlines MNC 487/8W arrived in January 1996, receiving dateless registrations in February. BVR 100T and KDB 137V followed in September via Barry Cooper, along with BVR 68T which was used for parts. They came from GM South's Birkenhead & District operation that had been a retaliatory response to Merseyside Transport's incursion into Greater Manchester. The buses went on to serve in Warrington from 2001-6. (MH)

Seven Leyland Atlanteans came from Stagecoach Manchester in 1996/7, with SND 479X used for parts. NIL 8256, previously SND 483X, has just arrived in Manchester on service 220, its displays set for the next departure to Droylsden. The Atlanteans were withdrawn in 1999/2000, with two moving to Warrington until 2003. (PM)

Scanias 1-4 had East Lancs new Cityzen bodywork and entered service in August and September 1996. The 76-seaters launched a Premier Service charter that promised modern buses on specific journeys and a free ride if one ran more than 20 minutes late or was cancelled for reasons within their control. Number 3 is seen in the grounds of the new superstore, built on the former Christy's mill site in Droylsden. (BL)

# A DECADE SINCE BUS DE-REGULATION

The Mayne Group now operated 82 vehicles, employed over 150 staff and had a turnover of £5.3 million. Before deregulation only one vehicle was required to run the 213 on Sundays, now 25 were needed to operate services 57, 96, 108/9, 115, 169, 171, 177, 220, 231/3, 236, 263, 290, plus the Peak District 395/6 and 460. These would be joined by three year contracts to run the Sunday 167 (Manchester – Norden) from 2nd October 1996 and 375 (Stockport – Denton) from 30th November 1997.

Other groups had emerged through the privatisation of the municipal and state-owned bus companies. The largest of these, Stagecoach, acquired GM South in February 1996. First, who now owned PMT, Pennine and Yorkshire Rider, bought GM North in March; while British Bus, who owned the remnants of Bee Line, became part of the Cowie motor dealership in August, changing its name to Arriva in 1997. The groups began to consolidate and simplify their networks to create frequent services with discounted weekly tickets, as Mayne quietly followed in their wake, picking up some of the pieces.

The daytime service 221 (Manchester – Stalybridge) was replaced along Ashton Old Road on 2nd September 1996, providing a combined 30-minute frequency with service 220. They would be diverted in the off-peak to replace First Pennine along Chapel Hill in Dukinfield and Park Road in Stalybridge, as new service 222 from 29th March 1999. Mayne also replaced Pennine's anti-clockwise link between Ashton and Hartshead on 19th July but new service 334 did not prove viable and ceased eight months later.

Former Scania demonstrator M113 RNK is approaching Piccadilly on service 220 in 1996, its front displays already set for its next journey, with a Dormobile Mercedes of Dennis's behind on service 219. (JAS)

Another route, created to link the new Tesco supermarket in Droylsden with Sunnyside Road and Piccadilly, had started on 2nd June 1997. Service 230 operated every 15 minutes and replaced the off-peak journeys on the 231 that had been introduced in April 1993. Its frequency was later halved to enable them to partially replace Stagecoach's service 217 (Manchester - Ashton) on 22nd November 1999.

Six new Scanias joined the fleet in 1996/7, followed by six Dennis Darts in 1997/8 - including five low-floor versions for the 171/2. Mayne reintroduced buses on most Bank Holidays from Easter 1998, after a seven-year absence, and was the first to introduce low-floor double-deck buses in Tameside. The five Dennis Tridents entered service on 6th September 1999 just days after Pennine withdrew their competing services in Mossley. Another battle had been won and, with many old-established operators having disappeared, Mayne were once again a rare survivor.

Five Marshall-bodied Dennis Dart SLFs (Super Low Floor) entered service on 1st March 1998 on services 171/2, joining a step-entrance version (R24 YNC) that had been purchased seven months earlier for service 170. *(BL)*

With Scania not yet offering a low-floor double-deck chassis, their next order was for five Dennis Tridents with East Lancs new 82-seat Lolyne design. V125-9 DJA entered service on 1st September 1999, with number 29 loaned to Isle of Man Transport for three days. The maroon stripe indicated their wheelchair accessibility. *(HW)*

# Chapter 7: Changing Times

It seems incredible now that, as the millennium approached, less than half of UK households owned a mobile phone, the internet required a dial-up connection, and shops largely remained the preserve of the high street. Growing prosperity and new technology would increasingly change our everyday lives, however, and gradually affect Mayne's too.

The coach fleet now consisted of a mix of Leyland, Dennis and DAF-powered vehicles, as well as a pair of new Volvos and Scanias. Land adjoining Mayne Garage was acquired, followed by the neighbouring Carlton Bingo Hall that was demolished in May and June 1998. The Warrington business was renamed Mayne Coaches on 14th July, having moved its 28 vehicles to a new 2¼-acre site on Battersby Lane, close to the centre of the town.

Despite the popularity of the coach holidays, the low margins and considerable time needed to organise them could no longer be justified, so they stopped in early 1998. Although this removed the pick-up points in Trafford and Rochdale, those in Salford became part of the excursions programme in 1999, along with Peel Green, Monton, Prestwich and Crumpsall; whilst those in Dane Bank, Hattersley, Mossley, Middleton, Moston and Openshaw were dropped, reducing the total to 30.

Volvo acquired Leyland Bus in 1988 and ceased production of the Tiger chassis in 1992 in favour of the Swedish B10M. The Mayne Group purchased four of the latter in 1997 with Plaxton Premiere 320 coachwork - a design that had replaced the Paramount range in 1991. P75/6 JND were delivered to Manchester, the latter is seen leaving Manchester Velodrome. (JAS)

RAZ 5172 (D634 WNU) was one of six DAF MB230s acquired from Trent Barton in 1997/8. They had Plaxton Paramount 3200II coachwork and were operated until 2002/4. Number 72 is seen in Grasscroft on 16th June 2000, transporting a local brass band between venues in the annual Whit Friday Brass Band Contest. *(DF)*

Despite running Scania buses since 1989, it was not until September 1998 that the first Scania coach was purchased. This 9-litre L94 had coachwork from the Spanish manufacturer Irizar and was originally registered S63 TNA. It would be followed by four more in 1999, with two going to Warrington. *(DF)*

Joining the Scanias were two DAF-powered Bova Futuras, S57 TNA and T58 JDB. The 49-seat executive coaches replaced G57/8 SBA as the company's flagships. *(AC)*

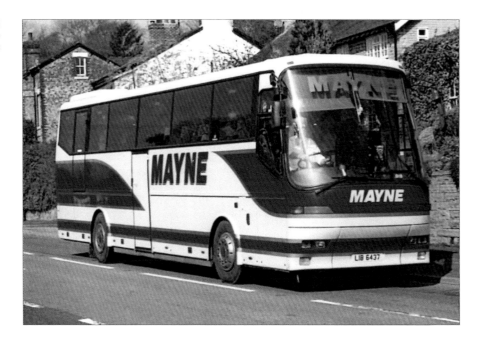

Blackpool, once the mecca of British holidays, had lost its crown to European resorts like Spain, exacerbated by a growth in cheap flights. The holiday service was replaced by regular excursions with the option of period return fares. The North Wales express continued however, serving Towyn, Prestatyn, Rhyl, Colwyn Bay and Llandudno every Saturday from July to September.

# INCREASING COSTS

The emergence of low-cost operators, not all of whom were doing things properly, began to increasingly affect Mayne's ability to win subsidised bus contracts. This, along with rising fuel and insurance costs, led to the loss of the 96, 108/9, 115, 169, 177, 263, 290/1, 396 and 460 in 1997/8. Despite running fewer buses on Sundays, they continued to operate a dozen school contracts, running 18 routes in Tameside and Manchester, alongside their commercial network and the subsidised services 170-2.

Service 395 to Castleton, which ran every Sunday from 2nd October 1997, was re-numbered 373 under revised Derbyshire County Council contracts from 4th April 1999, when Saturday journeys commenced on the 400/1 (Glossop - New Mills). A Yorkshire National Park contract also saw them provide a round trip between Manchester and Hawes on Sundays and Bank Holidays during July and August 2000. Service 821 ran via Bury, Burnley, Skipton and Grassington. Sunday journeys on the 196 were also briefly regained from 17th September under a six-month contract.

Two more East Lancs/Scania double-deckers (X118/9 YBA) entered service in September, followed by the first of 12 examples from Brighton & Hove in April 2001. Mayne's 33 buses now covered some 1.9 million miles a year, but soaring fuel prices, along with a new European directive that increased staff and pension costs, began to hit the company hard. Services 221/2 were withdrawn from 7th January 2001 and the evening journeys on the 220 and 231 became subsidised by GMPTE. Mayne also stopped selling fuel on 28th July after 62½ years, deciding they could no longer compete with supermarket prices.

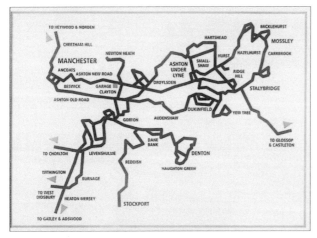

*Left:* **The Mayne bus network circa 2000 showing its core routes along the two Ashton roads and the subsidised bus contract work that continued to take their vehicles much further afield. (Mayne)**

*Below left:* **Number 24 is seen in Newton Street, Manchester preparing for the 09.00 Sunday departure to Castleton in the Peak District.** *(PM)*

*Below right:* **Numbers 18 & 19 were amongst the last Scania N113 to enter service in the UK in September 2000, as legislation required all new buses to be wheelchair accessible from the end of the year. The pair replaced Atlanteans and would be part-exchanged for new Scania coaches in April 2004, later passing to Holmeswood.** *(PM)*

The last Leopard came from Trent Barton, entering service on a school contract in September 1996. Number 61 is seen here with the former Brighton & Hove Javelin, G509 SAP. At least three Mayne Leopards (HDB 355V and SNC 365/6X) were still in existence in 2022, some 13 years after the last (366) was retired. (HW)

Five Volvo B7Rs with Plaxton Prima coachwork were delivered in March 2000, along with two B10Ms from a cancelled Arriva order. Three of the 7-litre B7Rs, W81-3 JBN, were based at Clayton. (Mayne)

Having tried to buy some East Lancs Scania N112 from Stagecoach Hull in May 1999, four were eventually acquired from Brighton & Hove in April 2001. C110-3 UBC were new to Leicester City Bus and had their flat windscreens replaced with this more concave version by Brighton in 1989. Initially numbered 20-3, they moved to Warrington in May 2002, where they would serve for several more years as numbers 10-3. (BL)

The Scanias were replaced at Manchester by eight more Brighton Scanias in April and May 2002, of which seven entered service and received fleet livery. E701 & 6 EFG (20/3) are seen above right on Manor Road in July 2002. Number 20 would be sold seven months later and has been preserved as a Brighton & Hove bus. (BL)

Eleven Scania N113s were purchased in 2003/4, with most sold on to either PC Coaches of Lincoln or Scania for new coaches. Only one entered service. F716 LFG became fleet number 20 on 8th August 2003 and is seen here in Piccadilly operating a journey on the 233 to Carrbrook. (PM)

Two of the Plaxton DAFs (52 & 73) were part-exchanged for new Scania K114 (YS02 XDW/X), with Irizar InterCentury coachwork in July 2002. Numbered 51/2, they had Scania DC11 engines as did the bus fleet and were operated until June 2016. *(PM)*

Another 10-litre Scania K114 arrived in May 2003. Number 53 was originally YS03 WRW and seen here providing transport for the Whit Friday Brass Band Contest on 1st June 2012. It was sold to Lloyd Coaches, Machynlleth in June 2016, along with siblings 51/2. *(DF)*

Two low-floor Dennis Tridents entered service in March 2003. MX03 KZN/P (30/1) had Plaxton President bodywork — a design that was launched in 1997 after Plaxton's acquisition of Northern Counties. *(BL)*

## COMMONWEALTH GAMES

In a further attempt to regenerate East Manchester, plans were announced in 1993 to build a sports stadium on the site of the former colliery as part of Manchester's bid to host the 2000 Summer Olympics. Although they lost out to Sydney, it did not deter the council from bidding for the Millennium Stadium rights, nor the 2002 Commonwealth Games for which it was finally successful.

The Games, held between 25th July and 4th August, led to a £68,000 contract to provide part of a shuttle service between Manchester's Victoria Station and the Stadium, requiring seven double-deck buses, plus extra Sunday morning journeys on the 231 and 236, with standby vehicles supplied by their Warrington associate.

Services 217 and 230 were diverted in Beswick via Alan Turing Way, Hulme Hall Lane and Bradford Road from 9th June to improve links with a new Asda superstore. The facility was another cornerstone in the regeneration, along with a cycling velodrome on the site of the old power station. Changes to the road layout in Manchester enabled the 232-5 to move to Cannon Street from 1st September 2002, when the Sunday 236 was reduced to hourly.

An agency began selling advertising space on the buses from October to help boost revenue. However, an arson attack at the Fairclough Street yard in November destroyed three coaches (Leyland Tigers B350 RNA, C347 YBA, and Volvo P75 JND) at a cost of nearly £78,000. Thankfully, the new Scania coaches (YS02 XDW/X) were spared. Another arrived in 2003 (YN03 WRW), joining two low-floor Dennis Trident double-deckers (MX03 KZN/P).

## CHANGING LOYALTIES

Competition between Stagecoach and Dennis's on the two Ashton roads had become fierce. With weekly tickets costing less than £10 and Stagecoach utilising its low-cost Magic Bus concept, Mayne's return fares now held little attraction on the common sections of route.

With patronage and profits falling, services 217 and 220 ceased on 23rd February 2004, followed by service 230 on 25th July. GMPTE sought a replacement for the 217, with one journey an hour diverted via the 220 route between Audenshaw, Dukinfield and Tameside Hospital, as new service 218. Mayne won the contract, hoping it would bring some stability to their network, as plans to extend Metrolink hit the buffers due to escalating costs.

Two new Scania/East Lancs single-deckers arrived in January 2004 (YN53 PCV/ GFJ), followed by three Dennis Darts from Brighton & Hove and the first of four 10-year-old Scania single-deckers. Olive Mayne retired as the Group's company secretary on 1st November 2004 after 47 years, with Stephen's wife, Diane, taking on this important role.

Scania introduced its low-floor N94UB chassis in 2003. Two single-deck examples were built with East Lancs Myllenium bodywork and entered service in January 2004. YN53 PCV/GFJ became numbers 40 and 41. The 35-seaters were the last new buses purchased by Mayne. (HW)

Stagecoach acquired Dennis's on 31st March 2005 and increased the 216 to every 5 minutes, leaving little room for Mayne. Services 232-5 moved to Manchester's new Shudehill Interchange on 29th January 2006. A round-trip via Mossley now covered 47 miles and sewer works in Manchester started to wreak havoc with their punctuality.

GMPTE introduced free off-peak concessionary travel in April, further affecting Mayne's income, and secured funding to extend Metrolink to Droylsden in July. The route, later extended to Ashton, would run along much of Ashton New Road, requiring significant works to move utilities out of its path. Mayne increased its resources and journey times from 4th September and extended the 217 and 231 to Shudehill, as running buses continued to get harder and more expensive.

After considering plans to combine the Manchester depots onto a site on Clayton Lane, the garage and land on Ashton New Road was sold for almost £1.2m, with the deal requiring completion within a year. The passing of Stephen's mother on 4th August 2006, along with indications that his children - Tina, Chris and Sarah - did not want to work in the business, led him to begin considering the Group's future.

Services 233/5 were withdrawn in the off-peak and on Saturdays on 29th January 2007, reducing the Ashton to Mossley circulars to every hour. The section between Manchester and Ashton was replaced by two journeys an hour, numbered 230 to maintain a core 15 minute service through Droylsden.

The company's 19 Manchester-based coaches moved to Mayne Coaches licence on 31st October 2007, along with 20 staff. It was then announced on 19th November, that the bus operation was being sold to Stagecoach. Manchester's oldest bus operator, having withstood numerous attempts to put an end to its activities, had finally succumbed to the changing times.

Three 8.5m Dennis Darts with Wright bodywork were purchased from Brighton & Hove on 8th April 2004. K129 LGO and NDZ 3160/1 were new to London Buses in 1992/3. Numbered 44, 18 and 19 with Mayne, number 18 was withdrawn in 2007 and the other two were sold by Stagecoach to GHA in 2008. (PM)

The last vehicle purchased by A Mayne & Son Ltd was this Scania L113 with Wright bodywork. It was new to Bullocks of Cheadle and one of the first low floor buses introduced in Greater Manchester in 1995. Seen here on 28th December 2007, number 36 joined the former demonstrator M113 SLS (37) and M521/2 UTV (38/9) purchased from Nottingham in March 2005. (HW)

# TERMINUS

Stagecoach's market dominance meant that the deal required approval from the Office of Fair Trading. The sale of Mayne Garage meanwhile had to be completed by 31st December, forcing them to rent temporary parking facilities at the Velodrome, creating further challenges for the family concern.

The OFT concluded on 10th January 2008 that Mayne's departure was unlikely to diminish competition in the area, enabling the sale to take place eleven days later. Thirty-seven vehicles, including 20 Scanias, seven Dennis Tridents, nine Dennis Darts, plus a recovery truck, eventually moved to Stagecoach's depots at Hyde Road and Glossop on 28th January, along with 122 staff. Initially run separately, its services and contracts migrated to Stagecoach Manchester's licence on 22nd June. Services 230-5 were replaced by a revised 231 (Manchester – Ashton via Hartshead and Tameside Hospital) from 26th October, as the older buses were withdrawn, and the low-floor vehicles began to move elsewhere.

The enduring company would have one last hurrah though when Stagecoach acquired First's services in Wigan on 3rd December 2012. The former Mayne business ran under the trading name of Stagecoach Wigan until 25th October 2015. It then lay dormant until being dissolved on 19th June 2018, almost 100 years since Arthur's career was changed by war, and thoughts of running a transport business had taken root.

Manchester's bus network continued to consolidate, with companies such as Bullocks and Finglands pulling out, gradually reducing the number of operators to around 30. With local politicians considering deregulation a failure, a return to a more integrated system is once again on the cards. At a public meeting to outline the benefits of a franchised network in 2019, the audience were asked to name a good bus company. Perhaps unsurprisingly many mentioned Mayne. Despite not running local buses for over a decade, their friendly, reliable services have not been forgotten.

Scania number 10, now Stagecoach's 15382, was the first to be repainted in March 2008 and withdrawn in 2009. Reinstated for use by their new depot at Ashton, it was later scrapped along with four other Scanias in 2011 but some of those that were sold before the takeover were still running some ten years later. *(BL)*

# CHAPTER 8: WARRINGTON

Although the bus operation had been sold, Mayne's coach hire business continued from bases in Clayton and Warrington. There are many parallels in the history of the two, with Warrington having also been a centre for wire, textiles and chemicals. Following a decline in the 1970's, the growth of the new town around Warrington led to an increase in employment in light industry, distribution and technology.

It was these prospects that probably encouraged Stephen Mayne to invest in the Barry Cooper business and seek to develop it further. The fleet acquired in 1982 consisted of 19 Leyland Leopards, four Volvo B58s and two Bedford SB5s, mostly with Plaxton coachwork. The offices were a former house at 110 Grappenhall Road that had a large yard and workshop at the rear, off Lumb Brook Road, plus Naylor's former base at Sandy Lane.

The Volvos and Bedfords were replaced with five new Leyland Tigers and a Bedford PJK in 1983/4, introducing the red and cream colours of Mayne, who provided its accounts and payroll functions, along with a £160,000 loan. Stephen divided his time between the two companies and even encouraged a degree of rivalry between them in the interest of improving profitability. The separate entities also meant that invoices would be raised whenever any help was given. Cooper's engineer, Rob Vernon – who had overseen the modification and rebuilding of several of the Leopards – later became General Manager, assisted by Amanda Jackson, who would eventually become managing director in 2015.

The first of five new Leyland Tigers delivered in 1983 was A418 HND, later YPL 764, seen here at the Sandy Lane depot in Stockton Heath in 1995 alongside a 1980 Leopard that was formerly HDB 357V. *(MH)*

## GROWING THE FLEET

The Warrington fleet was kept busy operating school and works contracts, along with private hires and day excursions, while the newest vehicles were usually employed on corporate hire and tour work for companies such as Schools Abroad and Pendle Travel, later known as Airtours. Three more Plaxton/Tigers were purchased in 1985/6, increasing the Executive coaches to two. These were followed by the first of five Leopards from Mayne and several more from PMT and West Yorkshire PTE. Services also began to the Manchester Grammar Schools.

The contracts and five Bedfords of Lymmville Coaches were acquired in January 1988. Subsidised bus contracts were also run in Warrington for Cheshire County Council on services 3, 24A and 91 (to Martinscroft, Risley Moss and Dallam) for a year; as well as shoppers and weekend journeys in Northwich, Prescot and Widnes until October 1992, by which time they were increasingly focusing on tour work, notably to Euro Disney.

*Top left:* This Bedford YRQ with Duple Dominant II coachwork was one of five similar vehicles acquired with the contracts of Lymmville Coaches in January 1988. The business was founded in 1968 by William Yoxall, who entered into a partnership with Ray Armstrong in May 1970 before selling him the firm in January 1975. *(DF)*

*Top right:* Further Leyland Tigers were delivered in March 1985 and 1986. B424/5 RNA (24/5, later 16/7) were 3.2m-high Plaxton Paramount 3200II, while C426 YBA (26) was a Gardner-powered 3.5m executive 3500II. Number 26, seen here at Wembley, was re-registered LIB 6440 in October 1988 and operated until January 1999. *(PM)*

*Centre left:* This DAF SB230 with Duple 320 coachwork was delivered in January 1989 and operated until January 1997. The 57-seater is pictured at the Grand National on 8th April 1989. *(DF)*

*Centre right:* Two 11m-Dennis Javelin were purchased in 1991. H28 FVM entered service in April, followed by J29 LJA in August. The 55-seaters were operated until December 1998. *(DF)*

*Right:* Leopards were the mainstay of the fleet for many years. This example, formerly HDB 356V, was one of the first to move from Clayton to Stockton Heath in 1985 and operated until 1999. The first Barry Cooper coach to move to Mayne was the Duple re-body ASV 764 that was fittingly the last operational example to return in 2000. *(MH)*

Some of Mayne's double-deck buses were used on rail replacement work in Warrington during 1994 and on school contracts from September. Their premises in Stockton Heath were sold for redevelopment, resulting in the move to a 2¼-acre site on Battersby Lane in central Warrington on 20th February 1998. The former British Road Services base was built in the 1950s to serve the neighbouring Rylands wire works.

The Mayne Coaches name was adopted on 14th July. They were operating 28 vehicles by the turn of the Millennium, including nine double-deckers (all Fleetlines), six Leyland Leopards, three Tigers, six Volvo B10Ms and two B7Rs, mostly with Plaxton coachwork. There were also two Scania L94s with Irizar coachwork from the Basque region of Spain. More Scanias would follow, along with several mid-life Dennis, Volvo and Bova Futuras, gradually increasing the fleet to 32.

Barry Cooper ran an AEC Regent (KDJ 999) and then a PDR1 Atlantean (KCN 184) on school contracts in the 1970s, but it would be 1994 before double-deck buses made a proper comeback, with YNA 328M being one of four initially operated. *(MH)*

An order for two Volvo B10Ms with Plaxton Premiere 320 coachwork in 1997 (P121/2 JNF) was repeated in 1998 with R119/20 CNE. Number 21 is pictured at the Lumb Brook Road yard prior to entering service in April. *(MH)*

Four more Volvos were delivered in 2000 (W425-8 JBU). Numbers 27/8 were from a cancelled Arriva order and were later up-seated to 70 in a two-plus-three seat layout. *(DF)*

Scania L94s T223/4 JND were delivered in May 1999 with 55-seat Irizar InterCentury coachwork and originally wore the same livery as Volvos 25-8. Number 24 inherited the registration ASV 764 in December 2002. (Mayne)

YN06 JXF was one of three Scania K114 for the Warrington operation in April 2006. (Mayne)

The new depot and office building on Marsh House Lane was originally part of a potential plan to consolidate the four Mayne Group premises into two modern, purpose-built facilities. (Mayne)

## CONSOLIDATION

The Warrington depot was sold for redevelopment as housing in March 2006, enabling a move to a new, purpose-built facility on an adjacent site. The new depot on Marsh House Lane opened on 4th December, with a two-storey office building, the upper floor of which is rented out, a heated and well-lit workshop that can accommodate six 14-metre vehicles, and ample parking outside for its fleet.

The Warrington licence was increased to 40 vehicles in 2007 to accommodate the Group's Manchester coach operation, which was transferred at the end of October, along with 20 staff and premises at Fairclough Street in Clayton. The family's long history in the coach travel business was therefore brought together under a single entity.

Vehicle manufacturer Alexander Dennis acquired Plaxton in May 2007. Two Dennis Javelins with Plaxton Profile coachwork (YN57 BWX/Y) were delivered four months later, numbered 26/7. The latter is pictured with J26 JHT, an Alexander-bodied Leyland Olympian that was new to China Light & Power of Hong Kong in 1992. The 100-seat, tri-axle was purchased from Morton's Travel in May 2014 in whose colours it remained. (Mayne)

The first new coach delivered after the sale of the bus operation was this Scania K340 with 49-seat Irizar PB executive bodywork. Number 60 entered service in March 2009 and was operated until 2012. (PM)

The Irizar was followed by four Scania K310s with 59-seat Irizar i4 coachwork. Numbered 54/5 and 61/2, they were initially based at Clayton. Number 62 is seen here carrying Manchester City fans to a Wembley cup final. (PM)

Mayne's ancestral home in East Manchester meanwhile continued to be redeveloped. A football academy and local amenities were built on the former Clayton Aniline site, near where Arthur and Matilda had started out in business all those years ago.

After buying two Dennis Javelins in 2007 (YN57 BWX/Y), Mayne began favouring Scanias, buying five new Irizar i4s in 2009/11, two new OmniExpress in 2010 and seven Irizar PB's from 2007-12. The school buses were also gradually replaced, with the capacity of some of the older coaches being increased to seat 68-70 passengers.

# RECESSION

A global economic crisis led to recession in 2008. This, coupled with the loss of the advertising and presence the bus fleet had provided, began to affect the excursions programme. Metrolink construction also increased journey times on its four feeder routes. The holiday express service to North Wales ceased in 2009 after 43 years. Although reinstated in 2011 due to demand, its viability again forced its cancellation in 2013.

A £250,000 contract to supply transport for Bury College was won in September 2011, with ten routes initially operated across Bolton, Bury, Rochdale and north Manchester occupying much of the Manchester fleet until the last of the contracts expired in July 2019.

The industry was saddened to learn that Stephen Mayne had died on 28th July 2012, at the age of just 62. Although his shareholding passed to his children, it was his express wish that the company continue and achieve its centenary.

The Omni Express was a semi-integral coach built by Scania in partnership with the Finnish manufacturer Lahden from 2007 until 2013. Mayne took delivery of two 55-seat K360s in September 2010. YT60 OSM/N were numbered 59 and 56 respectively. *(Mayne)*

YT11 LRF was the fifth Irizar i4 to join the fleet, entering service in March 2011 in this unique colour scheme. *(Mayne)*

Four Scania K114 Irizar PBs were purchased from Veolia in August 2011, after the loss of its National Express contract work in March. OED 201 was originally YN05 WJU and is seen here in the yard at Marsh House Lane, with the spacious, modern workshops visible in the background. *(Mayne)*

A tri-axle Scania K400 Irizar PB entered service in October 2012 on corporate hire and third-party tour work. YT62 JCJ did not carry a fleet number and is seen here working for Newmarket Holidays. Its stay in the fleet was relatively short-lived as it was sold in November 2015. *(PM)*

Number 14 was the first new Plaxton to be purchased by Mayne since 2007, their first wheelchair accessible coach and also the first to introduce this bold new livery on 14th March 2014. *(Mayne)*

The first wheelchair-accessible coach arrived in 2014. The Plaxton Volvo B9R (YX14 SEY) introduced a striking new all-red livery, designed by Diane Mayne and Amanda Jackson. Three Plaxton Panthers followed, including two from Matthews of Inniskeen, and the first of several new Plaxton Leopards.

The Manchester feeder routes were halved in 2015, with pick-ups retained in Gorton, Denton, Hyde, Stalybridge, Droylsden and Clayton; and Pendleton, Eccles, Swinton, Pendlebury, Blackley, Hollinwood, Failsworth and Newton Heath. The booking process also largely moved online, ending the agency arrangements that Matilda helped establish in the 1920s. Despite the ease in which bookings could now be made, however, people continued to forgo the luxury of days out. This led to the excursions ceasing in 2017 before demand again encouraged their reintroduction from Warrington in 2019.

With traditional contract work losing value, as competitors reduced rates in response to local government austerity, the company gradually trimmed its fleet from 47 to 36 vehicles, with around 10 based in Manchester. They also broadened their horizons and sought more profitable work. Transfers and excursions for cruise lines, along with tours for specialist travel companies increasingly found favour alongside corporate, educational and group hires. Two luxurious Van Hool Altano coaches were acquired for this purpose in 2017/18, increasing the wheelchair accessible coaches to three. These were followed by a trio of accessible Volvo/ Plaxton Elites in 2019, by which time the fleet had reduced to 30, following a further decline in work at the Manchester yard.

This 53-seat Volvo B11R Plaxton Panther 3, entered service on 4th December 2014 as YX64 WBO. *(Mayne)*

Seven new Volvo B8R Plaxton Leopards were purchased between 2015 and 2018, with seating capacities ranging from 57 through to 72. Number 10 is one of two delivered on 31st May 2018 with 72-seats. It is seen in the Fairclough Street yard alongside Volvo B10M number 78 (P76 JND, EUK 978) and a Scania i4. *(Mayne)*

Two Volvo B9R Plaxton Panther 2s entered service in 2014, becoming numbers 33 and 34. The 53-seaters were new to Matthews of Inniskeen (Ireland) and became YN09 TOH and YN59 SVW on return to the UK. Number 33 is seen here on Peter Street in Manchester on 4th February 2015. *(HW)*

## UNPRECEDENTED TIMES

As concerns for our planet grew, the next challenge was thought to be meeting the latest emission standards to enable their fleet to remain part of the solution. Little did anyone realise, however, that a much greater challenge was on the horizon.

With an expanded list of day trips and dozens of group and educational tours planned, Mayne were anticipating a good centenary until the Coronavirus pandemic threw everything out of the window. With Government restrictions limiting the movement of people, their 28 vehicles were parked up at Marsh House Lane, the yard at Fairclough Street was mothballed and most of their staff were furloughed from 23rd March. The company was suddenly fighting for its future and felt forgotten by a government that considered coaches to be ineligible for the financial support being offered to the rest of the leisure and hospitality sector. It was to be an inglorious centenary for the family's transport business.

Although its school services continued, along with some excursions from 8th August, demand for private hires remained limited as the local population faced varying levels of restrictions. Further national lockdowns on 5th November 2020 and 6th January 2021, resulted in much of the fleet remaining inactive and the decision was taken to reduce it further and remove the Manchester yard from their operating licence.

Despite the gradual easing of restrictions from 8th March and an injection of further capital, Mayne Coaches recorded a loss of £430,900 in 2021. By January 2022, it was realised that the outlook was not sufficiently improving and it would not be possible to generate the funds needed to keep the business going for much longer.

Steps were taken to try and protect the remaining 15 staff through the creation of a new company, Mayne Travel Ltd on 11th February that could enable operations to continue as part of a pre-packaged administration deal. After approaching several potential buyers, no credible offer was received until the eleventh hour, when two were made for parts of the business as it entered administration on 14th February.

Two wheelchair accessible Van Hool TD921 Altano were acquired from Eavesway in 2017/18. The livery on 60 and 61 were slightly different, continuing the tradition established in the 1980s. (Mayne)

Go Goodwins of Eccles subsequently purchased the goodwill and bookings through acquiring Mayne Travel on 18th February for £20,000, with the vehicles and workshop equipment being sold to webuyanybus.com of Walsall for £80,000. The Mayne family retained ownership of the depots and premises through a holding company, that was established in 2016 but adopted the name of A Mayne & Son Ltd in April 2020.

The well-known name and coach bookings therefore passed to new owners after 102 years, along with some of the remaining coaches that were re-acquired. Although the new licence for Mayne Travel was not followed through, Go Goodwins has since re-opened the Clayton yard and briefly changed their company name to Mayne of Manchester Ltd, with plans to reintroduce the familiar red livery to their local bus routes. This clearly demonstrates Mayne's remarkable reputation, something the Mayne family and their employees can be justifiably proud of. Whatever the future now holds, it is hoped that Arthur's legacy will live on, and that people continue to enjoy travelling the Mayne way.

Three accessible Volvo B9R Plaxton Elite coaches arrived in June 2019. New to Parks of Hamilton in 2010, they were converted to seat 70 in 2018, becoming the first of the type to be certified to that capacity. Numbered 17, 22 and 25 in the Mayne fleet, two were painted cream with number 17 (SG60 KHP) painted red. (Mayne)

## Fleet History of A Mayne & Son

| Fleet No | Reg. No | Chassis | Number | Bodywork | Number | Capacity* | New | In | Out | Notes |
|---|---|---|---|---|---|---|---|---|---|---|
| | ND 435? | Fo'd Model T | | | | | 19?? | ?/20 | ?? | possibly NA 9763 |
| | ? | Dennis | | | | | 19?? | 4/20 | ?? | other 4-tonne petrol waggons were also possibly operated in this period |
| | ? | ? | | | | | ?? | ?? | ?? | |
| | ? | AEC Y - type | | | | | 19?? | ?/23 | ?/29 | |
| | NA 9673 | Halford or Belsize | | | | | 19?? | ?/24? | ?? | |
| | TW 634 | AEC 416 | | | | | 19?? | ?/25 | ?? | |
| | TW 1834 | AEC 509 | | | | | 19?? | ?/25 | ?? | |
| | VM 1279 | Dennis | | | | B20R | 1927 | ?/29 | by 37 | Ex Bryan, Higher Openshaw? |
| | VM 6225 | Crossley Eagle | | Warwick | | B30F | 1928 | 2/29 | ?? | Ex Ferrington |
| | VM 6226 | Crossley Eagle | | Warwick | | B30F | 1928 | 2/29 | ?? | Ex Ferrington |
| | VM 6227 | Crossley Eagle | | Warwick | | B30F | 1928 | 2/29 | ?? | Ex Ferrington. Body later used as staff canteen until 3/38 |
| | VR 498 | AEC Reliance 660 | | | | B32F | 1928 | 3/29 | ?? | |
| | FR 8956 | Leyland PLC1 | | | | C26? | 1928 | 4/31 | 8/33 | Ex Bracewell, Blackpool |
| | HD 2977 | Dennis E | | | | B32F | 1927 | 10/32 | 7/35 | Ex Yorkshire Woollen (55) |
| | VH 3225 | AEC Regal O662 | 662460 | Duple (rebody, originally Burlingham, B32R) | | C32F | 1930 | ?/32 | 5/47 | Ex Hanson, Huddersfield |
| | VH 3541 | AEC Regal O662 | 662617 | Duple (rebody, originally Burlingham, B32R) | | C32F | 1930 | ?/32 | ?/37 | Ex Hanson, Huddersfield |
| | XJ 5574 | AEC Regal O662 | 6621502 | Duple | 3279 | C32R | 1933 | 8/33 | ?/53 | Ex Yorkshire Woollen (95) |
| | HD 3433 | Dennis E | | | | B30F | 1928 | 12/33 | 12/36 | Ex United (AL416) as B28F |
| | AXJ 496 | AEC Regent O661 | 6612771 | Park Royal | | H32/28F | 1934 | 11/34 | 8/49 | Later converted to H33/29F |
| | BNF 553 | AEC Regent O661 | 6613576 | Park Royal | B3831 | H33/29F | 1935 | 8/35 | 3/59 | Rebodied by East Lancs in 1945 as H30/28F |
| | HD 2972 | Dernis E | | | | B30F | 1927 | 10/35 | 7/36 | Ex Yorkshire Woollen (53). Withdrawn 3/36 |
| | CNB 1 | AEC Regent O661 | 6613769 | Park Royal | B4103 | H33/29F | 1936 | 3/36 | 3/59 | Rebodied by East Lancs in 1945 as H30/28F |
| | SM 8353 | Albion PKA26 | | Albion | | B20F | 1930 | 7/36 | 11/39 | Ex United (AL416) as B28F |
| | CVR 1 | AEC Regent O661 | 6614415 | Park Royal | B4412 | H33/29F | 1936 | 9/36 | ?/59 | Rebodied by East Lancs in 1945 as H30/28F. Cvtd to towing waggon in 1955 |
| | HD 3438 | Dennis E | | | | B30F | 1927 | 3/37 | 10/37 | Ex Yorkshire Woollen (98). Withdrawn 6/37 |
| | DNC 156 | AEC Regal | 6622175 | Duple | 8594 | C32F | 1937 | 3/37 | 9/39 | Commandeered by Central Ordnance, Chilwell for war use |
| | DND 3 | AEC Regal | 6622178 | Duple | 8753 | C32F | 1937 | 5/37 | 9/39 | Commandeered for war use |
| | DNF 2 | AEC Regal | 6622181 | Duple | 8597 | C32F | 1937 | 6/37 | 9/39 | Commandeered for war use |
| | TV 735 | AEC Regent O661 | 661062 | EEC | | H27/24R | 1930 | 12/37 | 8/49 | Ex Nottingham (15). Rebodied by Park Royal (B5074) in 2/38 as H33/29F |
| | FJ 7821 | AEC Regent O661 | 6611575 | Brush (rebody) | | H33/28F | 1931 | ?/38 | ?/61 | Ex Exeter (23). Rebodied by East Lancs in 1943 as H30/28F |
| | BNF 773 | AEC Regal IV | 642037 | Duple (rebody, originally Harrington, C36F) | | C32F | 1935 | 7/38 | ?/53 | Bowker, Manchester |
| | AG 6021 | AEC Regal O662 | 662479 | Lansdowne (rebody, ex Porteous, B30F) | | C32F | 1931 | 7/40 | ?/52? | Ex Don, Southsea |
| | FV 1786 | AEC Regal O662 | | Burlingham | | C32F | 1931 | 7/40 | 9/52 | Ex Inman, Morecambe. Rebodied by Duple 10/47 |
| | GND 994 | Bedford OWB | 13454 | SMT | | B32F | 1943 | 4/43 | ?/49 | |

| Fleet No | Reg. No | Chassis | Number | Bodywork | Number | Capacity* | New | In | Out | Notes |
|---|---|---|---|---|---|---|---|---|---|---|
| | TV 4491 | AEC Regent O661 | 6611026 | Brush (originally Park Royal, H28/20R) | | H26/26R | 1931 | 9/45 | ?/50 | Ex Nottingham (100). |
| | TV 4945 | AEC Regent O661 | 6611697 | Brush (originally Park Royal, H28/20R) | | H26/26R | 1931 | 4/46 | ?/50 | Ex Nottingham (112). |
| 12 | HNE 2 | AEC Regal | 6625627 | Santus | | C33F | 1947 | 6/47 | 11/62 | Rebodied by Yeates to FC39F 1/54. To Dean 2/61. |
| 13 | HNE 3 | AEC Regal | 6625626 | Santus | | C33F | 1947 | 8/47 | 11/62 | Rebodied by Yeates to FC39F 1/54. To Dean 3/61. |
| | HF 9381 | Leyland TD3C | 4464 | Roe | GO4006 | H29/23C | 1934 | ?/47 | ?/47 | Ex Salford (1015) for parts |
| | HNE 512 | Bedford OB | 44784 | Duple Vista | | C29F | 1947 | 6/47 | 5/49 | |
| | HXJ 566 | AEC Regal III | O962210 | Bellhouse Hartwell | | C33F | 1947 | 9/47 | 2/59 | |
| | HXJ 567 | AEC Regal III | O962211 | Bellhouse Hartwell | | C33F | 1947 | 9/47 | 2/59 | |
| | JNC 3 | AEC Regal III | O962209 | Bellhouse Hartwell | | C33F | 1948 | 3/48 | 12/58 | |
| 16 | JNC 4 | AEC Regal III | O962212 | Bellhouse Hartwell | | C33F | 1948 | 6/48 | 12/60 | Fleet number from 1959. |
| | JND 404 | Bedford OB | 78906 | Duple Vista | 49740 | C29F | 1948 | 7/48 | ?/50 | |
| | KNA 876 | AEC Regent III O961 | 9612E2464 | East Lancs | 4448 | H33/26R | 1949 | 8/49 | ?/72 | used as staff canteen from 6/70, then sold & preserved briefly until c1975. |
| | KNA 877 | AEC Regent III O961 | 9612E2465 | East Lancs | 4447 | H33/26R | 1949 | 9/49 | 2/67 | |
| 17 | KVM 729 | Leyland Tiger PS2 | 494935 | Burlingham | 4218 | C33F | 1950 | ?/49 | 12/60 | Ex Harris, M/cr. |
| | KVR 320 | Bedford OB | 130575 | Duple Vista | 49741 | C29F | 1950 | 3/50 | 11/51 | |
| | AUM 407 | AEC Regent O661 | 6613214 | Roe (2/46, originally EEC) | GO2133 | H30/26R | 1935 | 10/50 | ?? | Ex Leeds (164). |
| | AUM 434 | AEC Regent O661 | 6613227 | Roe (1/46, originally EEC) | GO2137 | H30/26R | 1935 | 10/50 | ?/63 | Ex Leeds (191). |
| | RJ 8726 | AEC Regent O661 | 6615355 | Metro Cammell | | H26/22R | 1937 | ?/50 | ?/50 | Ex Salford (182) for parts |
| | RJ 8728 | AEC Regent O661 | 6615357 | Metro Cammell | | H26/22R | 1938 | ?/51 | 12/61 | Ex Salford (184). |
| | LXJ 318 | Bedford SB | 1058 | Mulliner | | B34F | 1951 | 7/51 | 6/55 | |
| | MNB 717 | Bedford SB | 5090 | Duple Vega | | C33F | 1951 | ?/51 | ?/56 | |
| | MNC 449 | Bedford SB | 4897 | Duple Vega | | C33F | 1952 | 2/52 | 6/57 | |
| | DGX 214 | AEC Regent O661 | 6614626 | LPTB | 16998 | H30/26R | 1936 | ?/52 | ?/56 | Ex London (STL1694). |
| | CUS 812 | AEC Regent O661 | 6616575 | Weymann | M2079 | H30/26R | 1939 | 1/53 | 4/62 | Ex Glasgow (647). |
| | CUS 818 | AEC Regent O661 | 6616581 | Weymann | M2085 | H30/26R | 1939 | 1/53 | 12/63 | Ex Glasgow (653). |
| | CXX 377 | AEC Regent O661 | 6614621 | LPTB | 16967 | H30/26R | 1936 | 11/53 | ?/54 | Ex London (STL1689). |
| 1 | JGE 334 | AEC Regal IV | 9821E268 | Yeates | 266 | C39C | 1951 | 1/54 | 1/67 | Ex Stewart, Glasgow. |
| 2 | HD 9304 | AEC Regal IV | 9821E281 | Plaxton | 1268 | C41C | 1952 | 1/54 | 12/59 | Ex Broadhead, Dewsbury. |
| | 7194 H | AEC Regent III 6813S | U163996 | Park Royal | B36807 | H30/26R | 1953 | 8/54 | 10/72 | Ex demonstrator. |
| | DGX 210 | AEC Regent O661 | 6614611 | LPTB | 16985 | H30/26R | 1936 | 9/54 | ?/55 | Ex London (STL1679). |
| | DGX 212 | AEC Regent O661 | 6614616 | LPTB | 17013 | H30/26R | 1936 | 10/54 | ?/55 | Ex London (STL1684). |
| 14 | RVM 70 | Bedford SBG | 37458 | Duple Vega | 1055/361 | C38F | 1955 | ?/55 | ?/63 | |
| | RNB 3 | Bedford SBG | 36437 | Duple Vega | 1055/216 | C38F | 1955 | ?/55 | 7/56 | |
| | RNB 4 | Bedford SBG | 35777 | Duple Vega | 1055/223 | C38F | 1955 | ?/55 | 9/57 | |
| | RNB 5 | Bedford SBG | 36654 | Duple Vega | 1055/257 | C38F | 1955 | 3/55 | by 59 | |
| 8 | SVM 3 | Bedford SBG | 44333 | Duple Vega | 1060/166 | C41F | 1956 | 4/56 | 1/63 | Survived in field until 2008/9. |
| 9 | SVM 4 | Bedford SBG | 44337 | Duple Vega | 1060/167 | C41F | 1956 | 4/56 | ?/63 | |
| 10 | SVM 5 | Bedford SBG | 44458 | Duple Vega | 1060/255 | C41F | 1956 | 4/56 | ?/63 | |
| | CUS 814 | AEC Regent O661 | 6616577 | Weymann | M2081 | H30/26R | 1939 | 5/56 | 12/63 | Ex Glasgow (649). Last with green light fitted next to destination display. |
| [3] | LBU 321 | AEC Reliance MU3R | MU3RV535 | Burlingham | 5806 | C41C | 1955 | 7/56 | 12/66 | Ex Holt, Oldham. |

89

| Fleet No | Reg. No | Chassis | Number | Bodywork | Number | Capacity* | New | In | Out | Notes |
|---|---|---|---|---|---|---|---|---|---|---|
| [4] | WH 3078 | Leyland TS1 | 61503 | Harrington (rebody, originally Duple) | | C31F | 1931 | 3/57 | 4/58 | From Dean, Newton Heath |
| [5] | HVU 112 | Leyland PS1/1 | 461194 | Burlingham | 2855 | C33F | 1947 | 3/57 | ?/61 | From Dean, Newton Heath |
| [6] | JNE 148 | Leyland PS1/1 | 418165 | Burlingham | 3122 | C33F | 1948 | 3/57 | 9/61 | From Dean, Newton Heath |
| [7] | KXJ 874 | Leyland PS1/1 | 500090 | Burlingham | 4101 | C33F | 1950 | 3/57 | ?/61 | From Dean, Newton Heath |
| [8] | MVR 756 | Bedford SB | 10165 | Duple Vega | 1011/74 | C35F | 1952 | 3/57 | 3/61 | From Dean, Newton Heath |
| [9] 16 | RNA 632 | Bedford SBG | 36525 | Yeates Riviera III | 494 | C36F | 1955 | 3/57 | 5/61 | From Dean, Newton Heath |
| | UNF 10 | AEC Regent V LD3RA | 406 | Park Royal | B40858 | H41/32R | 1957 | 7/57 | 9/76 | Withdrawn 6/76 |
| | UNF 11 | AEC Regent V LD3RA | 407 | Park Royal | B40859 | H41/32R | 1957 | 7/57 | 6/74 | |
| | UNF 12 | AEC Regent V LD3RA | 408 | Park Royal | B40860 | H41/32R | 1957 | 7/57 | 6/74 | |
| | FV 40 | Leyland TS1 | | Burlingham (1948 rebody) | | C33F | 1929 | 10/58 | 10/58 | From A. Lea, Audenshaw |
| 11 | SVM 407 | Bedford SBG | 45752 | Duple Super Vega | 1060/365 | C41F | 1956 | 10/58 | ?/63 | From A. Lea, Audenshaw |
| | DFV 77 | Seddon Mk4 | 3257 | KW | | C33F | 1949 | 10/58 | ?/59? | From A. Lea, Audenshaw |
| | FT 5711 | AEC Regent II | 7729 | Weymann | M2840 | H30/26R | 1946 | 12/58 | 12/67 | Ex Tynemouth (141) |
| 4 | XNB 13 | Bedford SB1 | 68685 | Duple Super Vega | 1105/255 | C41F | 1959 | 2/59 | 1/66 | |
| 5 | XNB 14 | Bedford SB1 | 68778 | Duple Super Vega | 1105/256 | C41F | 1959 | 2/59 | 2/67 | |
| 6 | XNB 15 | Bedford SB1 | 69693 | Duple Super Vega | 1105/257 | C41F | 1959 | 3/59 | 10/66 | |
| 7 | XNB 16 | Bedford SB1 | 69696 | Duple Super Vega | 1105/258 | C41F | 1959 | 3/59 | ?/66 | to Dean fleet 6/62 |
| | XNB 17 | Bedford SB1 | 69698 | Duple Super Vega | 1105/253 | C41F | 1959 | 3/59 | 2/66 | carried Dean titles |
| 15 | ATJ 511 | AEC Regal O662 | 6621937 | Plaxton (1949 rebody) | | FC33F | 1936 | 3/59 | ?? | Ex Stubbs, Miles Platting. Originally Burlingham C32F |
| | GUF 678 | Leyland Titan PD1 | 460791 | Park Royal | B32470 | H28/26R | 1946 | 12/59 | ?/65 | Ex Southdown |
| | ECY 874 | AEC Regent II | 8070 | Weymann | M2816 | H30/26R | 1947 | 6/60 | 11/65 | Ex South Wales (273) |
| 1 | 2244 NA | Bedford SB1 | 76558 | Duple Super Vega | 1120/248 | C41F | 1960 | ?/60 | 1/67 | |
| 2 | 2245 NA | Bedford SB1 | 76565 | Duple Super Vega | 1120/249 | C41F | 1960 | ?/60 | 1/67 | |
| | 4221 NC | Bedford SB1 | 85411 | Duple Super Vega | 1133/46 | C41F | 1961 | 2/61 | 9/68 | carried Dean titles |
| | 6972 ND | AEC Regent V 2D3RA | 1095 | Park Royal | B48681 | H41/32R | 1961 | 12/61 | 6/76 | |
| | 6973 ND | AEC Regent V 2D3RA | 1096 | Park Royal | B48682 | H41/32R | 1961 | 12/61 | 6/76 | |
| | 6974 ND | AEC Regent V 2D3RA | 1097 | Park Royal | B48683 | H41/32R | 1961 | 12/61 | 6/76 | |
| | 9085 ND | Bedford SB1 | 89539 | Plaxton Embassy I | 612816 | C41F | 1962 | 4/62 | 12/68 | |
| | 9086 ND | Bedford SB1 | 89540 | Plaxton Embassy I | 612817 | C41F | 1962 | 4/62 | 1/69 | |
| | 63 DBU | AEC Reliance 4MU3RA | 4091 | Plaxton Panorama | 622264 | C51F | 1962 | 3/63 | 6/70 | Ex demonstrator |
| | 2493 VM | Bedford SB5 | 91326 | Plaxton Embassy II | 622306 | C41F | 1963 | 4/63 | 11/69 | |
| | 2494 VM | Bedford SB5 | 91329 | Plaxton Embassy II | 622307 | C41F | 1963 | 4/63 | 11/69 | |
| | 2495 VM | Bedford SB5 | 91522 | Plaxton Embassy II | 632313 | C41F | 1963 | 4/63 | 5/69 | |
| | 2496 VM | Bedford SB5 | 91741 | Plaxton Embassy II | 632318 | C41F | 1963 | 4/63 | 11/70 | carried Dean titles |
| | 8859 VR | AEC Regent V 2D3RA | 1513 | East Lancs (Neepsend) | | H41/32R | 1963 | 1/64 | ?/08 | Withdrawn 11/80. Sold, then exported to Japan |
| | 8860 VR | AEC Regent V 2D3RA | 1514 | East Lancs (Neepsend) | | H41/32R | 1963 | 1/64 | 12/80 | Preserved in 1981 |
| | 291 HBU | Bedford SB5 | 94305 | Plaxton Embassy III | 642939 | C41F | 1964 | 3/64 | 12/70 | Dean titles |
| | 6352 VU | AEC Reliance 4MU3RA | 5404 | Plaxton Panorama | 642760 | C51F | 1964 | 3/64 | 11/71 | |
| | BNF 490C | Bedford VAL14 | 1527 | Plaxton Val | 652505 | C52F | 1965 | 2/65 | 11/72 | |
| | 540 ETE | Bedford SB8 | 61542 | Yeates Europa | 684 | C41F | 1958 | 3/65 | 2/66 | Ex County, Stockport |
| | BBU 958C | Bedford SB5 | 96200 | Plaxton Embassy IV | 652878 | C41F | 1965 | 3/65 | 5/71 | Dean titles |
| | BNF 491C | Bedford VAL14 | 1670 | Plaxton Val | 652518 | C52F | 1965 | 3/65 | 8/71 | |
| | BNF 492C | Bedford VAL14 | 1654 | Plaxton Val | 652519 | C52F | 1965 | 5/65 | ?/?? | |

| Fleet No | Reg. No | Chassis | Number | Bodywork | Number | Capacity* | New | In | Out | Notes |
|---|---|---|---|---|---|---|---|---|---|---|
| | DBU 646C | Bedford SB5 | 96491 | Plaxton Panorama | 653087 | C41F | 1965 | 6/65 | ?/72 | |
| | CXJ 520C | AEC Regent V 2D3RA | 1799 | Neepsend | | H41/32R | 1965 | 8/65 | 6/78 | |
| | CXJ 521C | AEC Regent V 2D3RA | 1800 | Neepsend | | H41/32R | 1965 | 8/65 | 6/78 | |
| | CXJ 522C | AEC Regent V 2D3RA | 1801 | Neepsend | | H41/32R | 1965 | 8/65 | 6/78 | |
| | ENE 454D | Bedford VAL14 | 6825332 | Plaxton Val | 669391 | C52F | 1966 | 4/66 | ?/75 | |
| | ENE 455D | Bedford VAL14 | 6826599 | Plaxton Val | 669392 | C52F | 1966 | 4/66 | ?/77 | |
| | GNF 812E | Bedford VAM14 | 6841383 | Plaxton Panorama I | 672127 | C45F | 1967 | 3/67 | 4/74 | |
| | GNF 813E | Bedford VAM14 | 6860146 | Plaxton Panorama I | 672130 | C45F | 1967 | 3/67 | 4/74 | |
| | GNF 814E | Bedford VAM14 | 6859681 | Plaxton Panorama I | 672132 | C45F | 1967 | 3/67 | 11/72 | |
| | GNF 815E | Bedford VAM14 | 6861666 | Plaxton Panorama I | 672133 | C45F | 1967 | 3/67 | 11/72? | |
| | GNF 816E | Bedford VAM14 | 6862031 | Plaxton Panorama I | 672135 | C45F | 1967 | 3/67 | 11/72? | |
| | GNF 817E | Bedford VAM14 | 6846419 | Plaxton Panorama I | 672136 | C45F | 1967 | 3/67 | 11/72? | |
| | TBU 7G | Bristol LHL6L | LHL-111 | Plaxton Panorama Elite | 693499 | C51F | 1969 | 4/69 | 11/76 | |
| | TBU 8G | Bristol LHL6L | LHL-120 | Plaxton Panorama Elite | 693500 | C51F | 1969 | 4/69 | 5/76 | |
| | TBU 9G | Bristol LHL6L | LHL-116 | Plaxton Panorama Elite | 693501 | C51F | 1969 | 4/69 | 11/76 | |
| | LVU 885G | Bedford VAL70 | 9T465356 | Plaxton Panorama Elite | 692467 | C52F | 1969 | 11/69 | ?/77 | Ex Mayfair, Wythenshawe |
| | WBU 714H | Bristol LH6L | LH-407 | Plaxton Panorama Elite | 709362 | C45F | 1970 | 5/70 | 4/78 | |
| | WBU 715H | Bristol LH6L | LH-454 | Plaxton Panorama Elite | 709361 | C45F | 1970 | 5/70 | 6/78 | |
| | BBU 37J | Bedford YRQ | OT482102 | Plaxton Panorama Elite II | 712240 | C45F | 1971 | 2/71 | 4/78 | |
| | BBU 38J | Bedford YRQ | OT482180 | Plaxton Panorama Elite II | 712245 | C45F | 1971 | 2/71 | 4/80 | |
| | MVM 824G | Bedford VAL70 | 9T466413 | Plaxton Panorama Elite | 692492 | C52F | 1969 | 10/71 | ?/77 | From Connelly, Gorton |
| | FBU 300K | Bedford YRQ | 2T471816 | Plaxton Panorama Elite II | 712240 | C45F | 1972 | 3/72 | 6/78 | |
| | FBU 301K | Bedford YRQ | 2T472028 | Plaxton Panorama Elite II | 712245 | C45F | 1972 | 3/72 | ?/78 | |
| | FBU 302K | AEC Reliance 6U3ZR | 7982 | Plaxton Elite Express II | 729701 | C51F | 1972 | 5/72 | 2/80 | |
| | FBU 303K | AEC Reliance 6U3ZR | 7983 | Plaxton Elite Express II | 729702 | C51F | 1972 | 5/72 | ?/79 | |
| | FBU 304K | AEC Reliance 6U3ZR | 7984 | Plaxton Elite Express II | 729703 | C51F | 1972 | 5/72 | 12/80 | |
| | FBU 305K | AEC Reliance 6U3ZR | 7985 | Plaxton Elite Express II | 729704 | C51F | 1972 | 5/72 | 10/78 | |
| | LBU 701L | Bedford SB5 | CW451634 | Plaxton Panorama IV | 73126 | C41F | 1973 | 3/73 | 6/80 | |
| | LBU 702L | Bedford SB5 | CW451659 | Plaxton Panorama IV | 73127 | C41F | 1973 | 3/73 | 2/79 | |
| | LBU 703L | Bedford SB5 | CW451887 | Plaxton Panorama IV | 73128 | C41F | 1973 | 5/73 | 5/79 | |
| | LBU 704L | Bedford SB5 | 2T476912 | Plaxton Panorama IV | 73125 | C41F | 1973 | 5/73 | 6/79 | |
| | FYG 775C | Bedford SB5 | 96658 | Duple | 160/28 | C41F | 1965 | 4/74 | ?/77 | From Morby, Droylsden |
| | KTJ 669C | Bedford VAL14 | 1574 | Plaxton Val | 652510 | C52F | 1965 | 4/74 | ?/77 | From Morby, Droylsden |
| | NKH 46 | Leyland Royal Tiger PSU11/15 | 515490 | Plaxton Venturer | 1715 | C41C | 1952 | 4/74 | ?/78 | From Morby, Droylsden (stored) |
| | WVU 829L | Ford Transit | | Williams | | C12F | 1973 | 12/74 | c3/82 | Ex Wilson, Failsworth |
| | HBA 696N | Bedford YRT | EW451760 | Plaxton Panorama Elite III | 7511TC087M | C53F | 1975 | 2/75 | ?/81 | |
| | KVU 60P | Bedford YRT | EW453220 | Plaxton Panorama Elite III | 7511TC151M | C53F | 1975 | 12/75 | 4/80 | |
| | KVU 61P | Bedford YRT | EW453096 | Plaxton Panorama Elite III | 7511TC152M | C53F | 1975 | 12/75 | 4/80 | |
| | KVU 62P | Bedford YRT | EW453190 | Plaxton Panorama Elite III | 7511TC153M | C53F | 1975 | 12/75 | 8/80 | |
| 10 | LRJ 210P | Daimler Fleetline CRG6LXB | 7600532 | Roe | GO7695 | H44/33F | 1976 | 6/76 | 11/90 | |
| 11 | LRJ 211P | Daimler Fleetline CRG6LXB | 7600533 | Roe | GO7696 | H44/33F | 1976 | 6/76 | 9/87 | |
| 12 | LRJ 212P | Daimler Fleetline CRG6LXB | 7600534 | Roe | GO7697 | H44/33F | 1976 | 6/76 | 11/88 | |
| 13 | LRJ 213P | Daimler Fleetline CRG6LXB | 7600535 | Roe | GO7698 | H44/33F | 1976 | 6/76 | 10/88 | |
| 14 | LRJ 214P | Daimler Fleetline CRG6LXB | 7600536 | Roe | GO7699 | H44/33F | 1976 | 6/76 | 9/88 | |
| | JCU 800G | Ford R226 | BC04JU53145 | Duple Northern Viceroy | 2017/7 | C53F | 1969 | 6/76 | 12/76 | Ex Wilson, Failsworth |

| Fleet No | Reg. No | Chassis | Number | Bodywork | Number | Capacity* | New | In | Out | Notes |
|---|---|---|---|---|---|---|---|---|---|---|
| | SBA 199R | Bedford YMT | GW454196 | Plaxton Supreme | 7711TCM226 | C53F | 1977 | 5/77 | ?/81 | |
| | SBA 200R | Bedford YMT | GW454062 | Plaxton Supreme | 7711TCM228 | C53F | 1977 | 6/77 | 6/80 | |
| | SBA 201R | Bedford YMT | GW453416 | Plaxton Supreme | 7711TCM227 | C53F | 1977 | 6/77 | 8/81 | |
| | SBA 202R | Bedford VAS5 | GW454685 | Plaxton Supreme | 77PJK049 | C29F | 1977 | 7/77 | 8/81 | |
| | VJA 660S | Bedford YMT | GW456090 | Plaxton Supreme | 7811TCM041 | C53F | 1978 | 1/78 | 7/82 | |
| | VJA 661S | Bedford YMT | HW452530 | Plaxton Supreme | 7811TCM117 | C53F | 1978 | 1/78 | 8/82 | |
| | VJA 663S | Bedford SB5 | HW451630 | Plaxton Supreme | 78NJM001 | C41F | 1978 | 3/78 | 3/84 | |
| | VJA 664S | Bedford SB5 | HW450850 | Plaxton Supreme | 78NJM002 | C41F | 1978 | 4/78 | 8/82 | |
| 16 | VJA 666S | Bristol VRT/SL3/6LXB | 1327 | Eastern Coach Works | 23452 | CH41/29F | 1978 | 4/78 | 10/89 | |
| 15 | VJA 665S | Bristol VRT/SL3/6LXB | 1328 | Eastern Coach Works | 23453 | CH41/29F | 1978 | 6/78 | 7/89 | |
| 17 | VJA 667S | Bristol VRT/SL3/6LXB | 1329 | Eastern Coach Works | 23454 | CH41/29F | 1978 | 6/78 | 7/89 | |
| | YNF 347T | Bedford YMT | HW452916 | Plaxton Supreme IV | 7811TC107 | C53F | 1978 | 8/78 | 5/82 | Intended as VJA662S. |
| | YNF 348T | Bedford YMT | HW455855 | Plaxton Supreme IV | 7811TC045 | C53F | 1978 | 8/78 | 11/81 | cream with red stripes |
| | YNF 349T | Bedford YMT | HW455968 | Plaxton Supreme IV | 7811TC??? | C53F | 1978 | 12/78 | ?/81 | cream with red stripes |
| | YNF 350T | Bedford SB5 | JW450265 | Duple Dominant I | 914/1452 | C41F | 1978 | 12/78 | 9/84 | |
| | YNF 351T | Bedford SB5 | JW450269 | Duple Dominant I | 914/1451 | C41F | 1978 | 12/78 | 4/83 | |
| | TNE 14K | Bedford SB5 | 2T471747 | Plaxton Panorama III | 728144 | C41F | 1972 | 7/79 | 9/79 | From Wood, Ashton-u-Lyne. |
| | TNE 15K | Bedford SB5 | 2T471770 | Plaxton Panorama III | 728143 | C41F | 1972 | 7/79 | 10/79 | From Wood, Ashton-u-Lyne. |
| | HDB 352V | Bedford YMT | JW458649 | Plaxton Supreme IV | 8011TC023 | C53F | 1980 | 2/80 | 2/82 | |
| | HDB 353V | Bedford YMT | JW458678 | Plaxton Supreme IV | 8011TC024 | C53F | 1980 | 2/80 | 2/82 | |
| 54 | HDB 354V | Leyland Leopard PSU3F/5R | 7903768 | Plaxton Supreme IV | 8011TL015 | C53F | 1980 | 2/80 | 4/86 | Became LJX 139 2/86. |
| 55 | HDB 355V | Leyland Leopard PSU3F/5R | 7903781 | Plaxton Supreme IV | 8011TL016 | C53F | 1980 | 2/80 | 8/87 | Became NMX 643 2/86. |
| 56 | HDB 356V | Leyland Leopard PSU5C/4R | 7904773 | Plaxton Supreme IV | 8012TC071 | C57F | 1980 | 5/80 | 7/85 | |
| 57 | HDB 357V | Leyland Leopard PSU5C/4R | 7904950 | Plaxton Supreme IV | 8012TC072 | C57F | 1980 | 5/80 | 7/85 | |
| 58/66 | MRJ 358V | Leyland Leopard PSU3F/4R | 7930019 | Plaxton Supreme IV Express | 8011LX584 | C53F | 1980 | 6/80 | c8/01 | MJI 5766 2/90. Front re-built after accident. |
| 8 | MRJ 8W | Bristol VRT/SL3/6LXB | 2449 | Eastern Coach Works | 24207 | CH41/29F | 1980 | 7/80 | 1/91 | |
| 9 | MRJ 9W | Bristol VRT/SL3/6LXB | 2450 | Eastern Coach Works | 24208 | CH41/29F | 1980 | 7/80 | 1/91 | |
| 59 | MRJ 359W | Leyland Leopard PSU5C/4R | 8030021 | Plaxton Supreme IV | 8112LC009 | C57F | 1981 | 4/81 | 1/97 | Became GIL 3259 4/90. |
| 60 | MRJ 360W | Leyland Leopard PSU5C/4R | 8030050 | Plaxton Supreme IV | 8112LC067 | C57F | 1981 | 4/81 | 5/98 | Became GIL 2160 3/90. |
| 61 | SNC 361X | Leyland Leopard PSU5C/4R | 7930137 | Plaxton Supreme IV | 8112LC072 | C57F | 1981 | 8/81 | 2/91 | Became NIB 3261 1/90. |
| 64 | SNC 364X | Leyland Leopard PSU5C/4R | 8030035 | Plaxton Supreme IV | 8112LC074 | C50F | 1981 | 8/81 | 10/97 | MJI 5764 2/90. Later C57F. |
| | LDJ 723W | Mercedes L207D | 601367-28.093993 | Devon Commercial | 58111M | M12 | 1980 | 8/81 | 4/87 | Ex O'Brien, Farnworth. |
| 52 | SND 352X | Leyland Tiger TRCTL11/3R | 8101748 | Plaxton Supreme VI Express | 8211LT56X502 | C53F | 1982 | 3/82 | 10/89 | Became MJI 5765 2/90. |
| 53 | SND 353X | Leyland Tiger TRCTL11/3R | 8102093 | Plaxton Supreme VI Express | 8211LT56X513 | C53F | 1982 | 3/82 | 10/89 | |
| 62 | SNC 362X | Leyland Leopard PSU5C/4R | 7930138 | Plaxton Supreme IV | 8112LC076 | C57F | 1982 | 4/82 | 9/06 | Became NIB 4162 4/90. |
| 66 | SNC 366X | Leyland Leopard PSU3A/5R | MM8101 (7001708) | Plaxton Supreme IV (4/82) | 8111LC054S | C53F | 1970 | 4/82 | 3/86 | Ex Midland Red North, WHA 236H, with Plaxton C49F body. Acquired by Barry Cooper 4/81 and rebuilt at Clayton. |
| 65 | SNC 365X | Leyland Leopard PSU5C/4R | 8030044 | Plaxton Supreme IV | 8112LC075 | C57F | 1982 | 4/82 | 3/97 | Became MJI 5765 2/90. |
| | PTO 350R | Leyland Leopard PSU5A/4R | 7602942 | Plaxton Supreme III | 7612LC035AM | C57F | 1976 | 6/82 | 5/83 | Ex Kettlewell, Retford |
| 63 | SNC 363X | Leyland Leopard PSU5C/4R | 8030016 | Plaxton Supreme IV | 8112LC073 | C57F | 1982 | 7/82 | 1/97 | Became MJI 5763 2/90. |
| 3 | OJD 163R | Leyland Fleetline FE30AGR | 7602788 | Park Royal | B60942 | H44/29F | 1976 | 11/82 | 8/96 | Ex London (DM2163). |
| 67 | ANA 367Y | Leyland Tiger TRCTL11/3R | 8200330 | Plaxton Paramount 3500 Exp | 8312LTH1X504 | C55F | 1983 | 3/83 | 2/93 | Became OJT 923 3/86. |
| 68/69 | ANA 368Y | Leyland Tiger TRCTL11/3R | 8200487 | Plaxton Paramount 3500 Exp | 8312LTH1X503 | C55F | 1983 | 3/83 | 1/00 | Became SSV 269 3/86. |
| 70 | A370 HNC | Leyland Tiger TRCTL11/3R | 8201498 | Plaxton Paramount 3500 | 8312LTH1C869 | C49Ft | 1983 | 9/83 | 10/99 | Became TKU 540 11/85. |
| 69 | A369 HNC | Leyland Tiger TRCTL11/3R | 8300086 | Plaxton Paramount 3500 | 8312LTH1C752 | C49F | 1984 | 3/84 | ?/86 | Became SXU 708 by 01/86. |

| Fleet No | Reg. No | Chassis | Number | Bodywork | Number | Capacity* | New | In | Out | Notes |
|---|---|---|---|---|---|---|---|---|---|---|
| 51 | A351 KBA | Bedford PJK | ET10097 | Plaxton Supreme IV | 848PJ54C002 | C29F | 1984 | 4/84 | 11/90 | |
| 1 | OJD 131R | Leyland Fleetline FE30AGR | 7601796 | Park Royal | B60910 | H44/29F | 1976 | 1/85 | 1/94 | Ex Stevensons, Uttoxeter |
| 5 | OUC 35R | Leyland Fleetline FE30ALR | 7601787 | Metro Cammell Weymann | | H45/32F | 1976 | 3/85 | 1/96 | Withdrawn 3/95 |
| 49/79 | B349 RNA | Leyland Tiger TRCTLXCT/3RZ | 8401076 | Plaxton Paramount 3200II | 8512LGP2C001 | C57F | 1985 | 5/85 | c7/02 | LIB 6439 10/88. Later C55F |
| 50 | B350 RNA | Leyland Tiger TRCTLXCT/3RZ | 8401195 | Plaxton Paramount 3200II | 8512LGP2C002 | C57F | 1985 | 5/85 | 11/02 | 403 BGO 6/87. To C55F 10/97 |
| 47/77 | C347 YBA | Leyland Tiger TRCTLXCT/3RZ | 8401210 | Plaxton Paramount 3500II | 8512LGH2C751 | C51Ft | 1986 | 3/86 | 11/02 | LIB 6437 10/88. C53F 10/97 |
| 48/78 | C348 YBA | Leyland Tiger TRCTLXCT/3RZ | 8401227 | Plaxton Paramount 3500II | 8512LGH2C752 | C51Ft | 1986 | 3/86 | 12/98 | Became LIB 6438 9/88 |
| 54 | ORO 325L | Leyland Leopard PSU5/4R (TL11) | 7102233 | Duple 320 (10/86) | 8590/0007 | C57F | 1973 | 9/86 | 1/00 | Ex Barry Cooper. Became ASV 764, 11/86 with TL11 engine. |
| | SCP 342L | Leyland Leopard PSU4B/2R | 7202389 | Plaxton Derwent | 729922 | B45F | 1972 | 3/87 | 10/87 | Ex West Yorkshire (3002) |
| 6 | UJX 916M | Leyland Leopard PSU4B/2R | 7302898 | Plaxton Derwent | 733995 | B45F | 1973 | 3/87 | 4/88 | Ex West Yorkshire (3006) |
| 4 | UJX 918M | Leyland Leopard PSU4B/2R | 7302900 | Plaxton Derwent | 743997 | B45F | 1973 | 3/87 | 11/88 | Ex West Yorkshire (3008) |
| 2 | GWY 692N | Leyland Leopard PSU4B/2R | 7604642 | Plaxton Derwent | 7410LB803S | B43F | 1975 | 3/87 | 12/88 | Ex West Yorkshire (3012) |
| 7 | JWU 252N | Leyland Leopard PSU4C/4R | 7501320 | Plaxton Derwent | 7510LB810 | B43F | 1975 | 3/87 | 12/88 | Ex West Yorkshire (8059) |
| 55 | GRF 267V | Leyland Leopard PSU3E/4R | 7902128 | Duple Dominant II Express | 934/5323 | C53F | 1979 | 5/87 | 12/87 | On loan from Barry Cooper |
| 18 | LJA 474P | Daimler Fleetline CRG6LXB | 65982 | Northern Counties | 7754 | H43/32F | 1975 | 7/87 | 9/93 | Ex GMT (7474) |
| 11 | LJA 470P | Daimler Fleetline CRG6LXB | 65984 | Northern Counties | 7750 | H43/32F | 1975 | 10/87 | 8/93 | Ex GMT (7470) |
| 19 | GWY 691N | Leyland Leopard PSU4B/2R | 7404641 | Plaxton Derwent | 7410LB802S | DP43F | 1975 | 10/87 | 12/88 | Ex Barry Cooper |
| 69 | GRF 267V | Leyland Leopard PSU3E/4R | 7902128 | Duple Dominant II Express | 934/5323 | C53F | 1979 | 10/88 | 3/89 | On loan from Barry Cooper |
| 4 | GND 505N | Daimler Fleetline CRG6LXB | 65952 | Northern Counties | 7719 | H43/32F | 1974 | 11/88 | 7/94 | Ex GMT (7439). |
| 6 | GNC 294N | Daimler Fleetline CRG6LXB | 65937 | Northern Counties | 7708 | H43/32F | 1974 | 11/88 | 7/92 | Ex GMT (7428) |
| 14 | GND 507N | Daimler Fleetline CRG6LXB | 65938 | Northern Counties | 7721 | H43/32F | 1974 | 11/88 | 2/92 | Ex GMT (7441). Withdrawn after low bridge accident |
| | WWH 62L | Daimler Fleetline CRG6LXB | 65697 | Northern Counties | 7530 | H43/32F | 1973 | 11/88 | 0/89 | Ex Smiths, Alcester |
| | YNA 306M | Daimler Fleetline CRG6LXB | 65831 | Northern Counties | 7631 | H43/32F | 1973 | 11/88 | 0/89 | Ex GMT (7351) |
| | YNA 315M | Daimler Fleetline CRG6LXB | 65890 | Northern Counties | 7640 | H43/32F | 1973 | 11/88 | 0/89 | Ex London, Harrow |
| 23 | NTX 361R | Leyland Leopard PSU3C/2R | 7603822 | Willowbrook | 76496 | B51F | 1976 | 11/88 | 2/91 | Ex Merthyr Tydfil (204). Became LIW 1324 in 10/90 |
| 24/25 | NTX 362R | Leyland Leopard PSU3C/2R | 7603871 | Willowbrook | 76497 | B51F | 1976 | 11/88 | 8/96 | Ex Merthyr Tydfil (205). Became NIB 7625 10/90. Rebodied as Willowbrook Warrior (90046), B48F 12/90 |
| 25/26 | NTX 363R | Leyland Leopard PSU3C/2R | 7604168 | Willowbrook | 76498 | B51F | 1976 | 11/88 | 2/91 | Ex Merthyr Tydfil (206) |
| 20 | BNE 735N | Daimler Fleetline CRG6LXB | 65915 | Northern Counties | 7699 | H43/32F | 1974 | 12/88 | 7/94 | Ex GMT (7419) |
| 21 | WWH 54L | Daimler Fleetline CRG6LXB | 65677 | Northern Counties | 7503 | H43/32F | 1973 | 12/88 | 3/91 | Ex GMT (7289) |
| 22/8 | YNA 328M | Daimler Fleetline CRG6LXB | 65898 | Northern Counties | 7653 | H43/32F | 1973 | 12/88 | 9/94 | Ex GMT (7373). |
| 19 | BNE 740N | Daimler Fleetline CRG6LXB | 65942 | Northern Counties | 7704 | H43/32F | 1974 | 12/88 | 0/91 | Ex GMT (7424). In use 8/89 |
| 69 | UWY 62X | Leyland Leopard PSU3C/4R | 8130185 | Duple Dominant IV Express | 134/5388 | C57F | 1981 | 1/89 | 1/90 | Ex West Yorkshire (new as UUM 49W). Wdn 10/89 |
| 55 | F55 HNC | Leyland Tiger TRCL10/3ARZM | TR00366 | Duple 340 | 8889/0826 | C53Ft | 1989 | 1/89 | 4/96 | Became IIL 1355 in 8/92 |
| 56 | F56 HNC | Leyland Tiger TRCL10/3RZA | TR00369 | Duple 320 | 8890/0849 | C57F | 1989 | 1/89 | 4/96 | Became IIL 1356 in 8/92 |
| 21 | WWH 24L | Daimler Fleetline CRG6LXB | 65775 | Park Royal | B59889 | H43/32F | 1973 | 2/89 | ?/89 | Ex Social Aid Council, Sale |
| | NTX 360R | Leyland Leopard PSU3C/2R | 7604063 | Willowbrook | 76495 | B51F | 1976 | 3/89 | ?/89 | Ex Merthyr Tydfil (203) |
| 12 | F112 HNC | Scania N113DRB | 1814756 | Northern Counties | 3768 | H47/32F | 1989 | 3/89 | SMR | Later H47/31F |
| | XJA 542L | Daimler Fleetline CRG6LXB | 65772 | Park Royal | B59886 | H43/32F | 1973 | 4/89 | ?/89 | Ex Gash, Newark |
| 13 | F113 HNC | Scania N113DRB | 1814763 | Northern Counties | 3769 | CH47/30F | 1989 | 5/89 | SMR | Later CH43/30F, then H47/31F |
| | C518 WBF | Leyland Tiger TRCTL11/3RZ | 8500786 | Duple 340 | 8595/0045 | C50Ft | 1986 | 5/89 | 8/89 | Ex Midland Red North (31) |
| | C520 WBF | Leyland Tiger TRCTL11/3RZ | 8500801 | Duple 340 | 8595/0047 | C50Ft | 1986 | 5/89 | 2/90 | Ex Midland Red North (32). |

93

| Fleet No | Reg. No | Chassis | Number | Bodywork | Number | Capacity* | New | In | Out | Notes |
|---|---|---|---|---|---|---|---|---|---|---|
| 2 | CSU 918 | Daimler Fleetline CRG6LXB | 65704 | Northern Counties | 7506 | H43/32F | 1974 | 8/89 | 10/91 | Ex (XJA 566L) Hulme Hall, Stockport. DRJ917L 9/91 |
| 15 | G115 SBA | Scania N113DRB | 1817457 | Northern Counties | 3770 | H47/32F | 1989 | 10/89 | SMR | |
| 69/24 | OWO 234Y | Leyland Leopard PSU3G/2R | 8230594 | Duple Dominant | 239/5627 | DP49F | 1982 | 11/89 | 4/93 | Ex Merthyr Tydfil (234) |
| 16 | G116 SBA | Scania N113DRB | 1814758 | Northern Counties | 3771 | H47/32F | 1989 | 12/89 | SMR | |
| 17 | G117 SBA | Scania N113DRB | 1814762 | Northern Counties | 3772 | H47/32F | 1989 | 2/90 | SMR(z) | Withdrawn by 2/06 (gearbox) |
| 57 | G57 SBA | Bova FHD 12.290 | 4524 | Bova Futura | - | C50Ft | 1990 | 2/90 | 10/98 | Became IIL 2257 in 08/92. |
| 58 | G58 SBA | Bova FHD 12.290 | 4525 | Bova Futura | - | C50Ft | 1990 | 2/90 | 12/98 | Became IIL 2258 in 08/92. Later C40Ft with tables |
| 7/27/41 | GDZ 3841 | Leyland Leopard PSU3B/4R | 7500796 | Willowbrook Warrior (11/89) | 88028 | B51F | 1975 | 2/90 | 9/99 | Ex Perry, Bromyard. Was Duple JVS928N (533/5115) until 12/89 |
| 22 | NRE 582L | Leyland Leopard PSU3B/4R | 7200912 | Willowbrook Warrior (12/90) | 90045 | B48F | 1973 | 5/90 | 2/96 | Ex Jowitt, Tankersley (chassis). LIW 1322 10/90. Withdrawn 11/95. RFM 186L 1/96 |
| 23 | RBF 987M | Ley and Leopard PSU3B/4R | 7304951 | Willowbrook Warrior (3/91) | 90050 | B48F | 1973 | 5/90 | 8/96 | Ex Jowitt, Tankersley (chassis), becoming LIW 1323 10/90 |
| | LBF 796L | Leyland Leopard PSU3C/4R | | - | - | | 1975 | 5/90 | ?/90 | Acquired as a chassis for re-bodying by Willowbrook (as LIW 1324) but was unsuitable and scrapped 12/90. |
| 10 | KUC 969P | Leyland Fleetline FE30AGR | 7600200 | Metro Cammell Weymann | | H45/32F | 1976 | 11/90 | 7/94 | Ex Wilts & Dorset. Cvtd to Garnder 6LXB |
| 26 | SSX 601V | Seddon Pennine VII | 70087 | Alexander AYS | 13AYS 2278/11 | B53F | 1980 | 1/91 | 8/93 | Ex Stevensons, Uttoxeter |
| 21 | A101 DPB | Dennis Falcon HS SDA407 | 142 | WS Vanguard (1987) | 1840/87 | DP49F | 1983 | 1/91 | 7/01 | Ex Wycombe. Wdn 9/99-9/00 |
| 7 | THX 322S | Leyland Fleetline FE30ALR Sp | 7702626 | Metro Cammell Weymann | | H44/24D | 1978 | 3/91 | 3/97 | Ex London (DMS2322). Later H44/31F |
| 9 | THX 579S | Leyland Fleetline FE30ALR Sp | 7704440 | Park Royal | B61178 | H44/24D | 1978 | 3/91 | 7/97 | Ex London (D2579). To H44/27F. Withdrawn 3/97 |
| | THX 496S | Leyland Fleetline FE30ALR Sp | 7701068 | Park Royal | B61095 | H44/24D | 1978 | 3/91 | 10/91 | Ex London (DMS2496) for parts |
| 28/33 | THX 303S | Leyland Fleetline FE30ALR Sp | 7702409 | Metro Cammell Weymann | | H44/24D | 1978 | 3/91 | 7/97 | Ex London (DMS2303). Cvtd to H44/31F. In service 8/92. Not used 7-12/95 |
| 29/35 | THX 555S | Leyland Fleetline FE30ALR Sp | 7703261 | Park Royal | B61154 | H44/31F | 1978 | 3/91 | 8/96 | Ex London (DMS2555). Cvtd to H44/31F. In service 12/91 |
| 31 | THX 601S | Leyland Fleetline FE30ALR Sp | 7703767 | Park Royal | B61200 | H44/31F | 1978 | 3/91 | 3/98 | Ex London (DM2601). Cvtd to H44/31F. In service 8/91? |
| 34 | THX 594S | Leyland Fleetline FE30ALR Sp | 7704839 | Park Royal | B61193 | H44/31F | 1978 | 3/91 | 3/98 | Ex London (DM2594). Cvtd to H44/31F. In service 8/91? |
| 35/2/35 | THX 515S | Leyland Fleetline FE30ALR Sp | 7701849 | Park Royal | B61114 | H44/31F | 1978 | 3/91 | 4/97 | Ex London (DMS2515). To H44/31F. In use 11/91-11/96 |
| 51 | H51 DVR | Dennis Javelin 8.5 SDA1915 | 431 | Duple 320 | 8884/0958 | C37F | 1991 | 3/91 | 1/02 | Later C35F. SIW 6251 8/96 |
| 52 | H52 FDB | Dennis Javelin 12 SDL1907 | 522 | Duple 320 | 8978/1156 | C55F | 1991 | 4/91 | 9/98 | Became PBZ 7052 in 3/97 |
| 53 | D323 RNS | Leyland Tiger TRCTL11/3RH | 8600509 | Duple 340 | 8695/0321 | C46Ft | 1987 | 9/91 | 9/94 | Ex Highland Scottish. Became HIL 6253 12/91 |
| 44 | A44 YWJ | Dennis Falcon HS SDA414 | 147 | Marshall Camair-80 | 270610 | DP53F | 1984 | 11/91 | 9/97 | Ex Chesterfield (44) |
| 45 | A45 YWJ | Dennis Falcon HS SDA414 | 148 | Marshall Camair-80 | 270611 | B53F | 1984 | 11/91 | 10/97 | Ex Chesterfield (45) |
| 46 | A46 YWJ | Dennis Falcon HS SDA414 | 149 | Marshall Camair-80 | 270612 | B53F | 1984 | 11/91 | 3/98 | Ex Chesterfield (46). Withdrawn 11/97 |
| 47 | A47 YWJ | Dennis Falcon HS SDA414 | 150 | Marshall Camair-80 | 270614 | B53F | 1984 | 11/91 | 3/98 | Ex Chesterfield (47). Wdn 1/98 |
| 48 | A48 YWJ | Dennis Falcon HS SDA414 | 151 | Marshall Camair-80 | 270613 | B53F | 1983 | 11/91 | 3/98 | Ex Chesterfield (48). Wdn 1/98 |
| | THX 564S | Leyland Fleetline FE30ALR Sp | 7703870 | Park Royal | B61163 | H44/24D | 1978 | 2/92 | 8/93 | Ex London (D2564). For parts |
| 19 | THX 619S | Leyland Fleetline FE30ALR Sp | 7705809 | Park Royal | B61218 | H44/31F | 1978 | 2/92 | 7/98 | Ex London (DM2619). Cvtd to H44/31F. Wdn 29/11/97 |

| Fleet No | Reg. No | Number | Chassis | Bodywork | Number | Capacity* | New | In | Out | Notes |
|---|---|---|---|---|---|---|---|---|---|---|
|  | THX 623S | 7705707 | Leyland Fleetline FE30ALR Sp | Park Royal | B61222 | H44/24D | 1978 | 2/92 | ?/92 | Ex London (D2623). For parts |
|  | THX 635S | 7800247 | Leyland Fleetline FE30ALR Sp | Park Royal | B61234 | H44/24D | 1978 | 2/92 | 11/92 | Ex London (D2635). For parts |
| 32 | GSC 857T | 7802778 | Leyland Fleetline FE30AGR | Eastern Coach Works | 23468 | H43/32F | 1979 | 11/92 | 9/95 | Ex Clydeside (804) |
| 6 | ULS 666T | 7806432 | Leyland Fleetline FE30AGR | Eastern Coach Works | 23594 | H43/32F | 1979 | 11/92 | 8/95 | Ex Clydeside (816) |
| 28 | K28 XBA | 1098 | Dennis Dart 9.8 SDL3012 | Marshall Dartline | C27.026 | B40F | 1992 | 11/92 | 2/98 |  |
| 30 | ULS 663T | 7806355 | Leyland Fleetline FE30AGR | Eastern Coach Works | 23583 | H43/32F | 1979 | 12/92 | 4/96 | Ex Clydeside (813) via Barry Cooper. Withdrawn 8/95 |
| 29 | K29 XBA | 1099 | Dennis Dart 9.8 SDL3012 | Marshall Dartline | C27.027 | B40F | 1992 | 1/93 | 2/98 |  |
| 36 | K36 XNE | 1101 | Dennis Dominator DDA2005 | East Lancs | B2601 | H45/31F | 1993 | 3/93 | 1/96 | Intended as Strathclyde K216 OGD |
| 37 | K37 XNE | 1102 | Dennis Dominator DDA2005 | East Lancs | B2603 | H45/31F | 1993 | 3/93 | 1/96 | Intended as Strathclyde K217 OGD |
| 38 | K38 YVM | 1103 | Dennis Dominator DDA2005 | East Lancs | B2602 | H45/31F | 1993 | 3/93 | 1/96 | Intended as Strathclyde K218 OGD |
| 14 | L114 DNA | 1821877 | Scania N113DRB | East Lancs | B6901 | H47/31F | 1993 | 8/93 | SMR | Intended as K114 XNE |
| 26 | L26 FNE | 1704 | Dennis Dart 9.8 SDL3035 | Marshall Dartline | C37.003 | B40F | 1994 | 2/94 | 2/98 |  |
| 27 | L27 FNE | 1705 | Dennis Dart 9.8 SDL3035 | Marshall Dartline | C37.004 | B40F | 1994 | 2/94 | 2/98 |  |
|  | ARB 134T | 7802231 | Leyland Leopard PSU3E/4R | Plaxton Supreme Express | 7811LXM527 | C49F | 1978 | 8/94 | 9/94 | Ex Trent/Barton (1345) |
|  | BRC 140T | 7806414 | Leyland Leopard PSU3E/4R | Plaxton Supreme Express | 7811LXM533 | C49F | 1979 | 8/94 | 9/94 | Ex Trent/Barton (140) |
|  | KVO 142W | 7930161 | Leyland Leopard PSU3E/4R | Willowbrook 003 | 7987 | C49F | 1980 | 8/94 | 1/95 | Ex Trent (142) |
| 24 | KVO 144W | 7930163 | Leyland Leopard PSU3E/4R | Willowbrook 003 | 79899 | C49F | 1980 | 8/94 | 10/97 | Ex Trent (144). Became LIL 9924 4/96. Withdrawn 4/97 |
| 40/22 | KVO 145W | 7930204 | Leyland Leopard PSU3E/4R | Willowbrook 003 | 79900 | C49F | 1981 | 8/94 | 5/98 | Ex Trent (145). In service 8/95. XIB 3922 6/96. Wdn 4/97  BTU 739W 6/97 |
|  | KVO 146W | 7930205 | Leyland Leopard PSU3E/4R | Willowbrook 003 | 79901 | C49F | 1981 | 8/94 | 12/94 | Ex Trent (146). Intended for re-bodying by East Lancs but later scrapped |
|  | THX 593S | 7705189 | Leyland Fleetline FE30ALR Sp | Park Royal | B61192 | H44/27D | 1978 | 11/94 | 4/96 | Ex Arkleston, Renfrew. Wdn 12/95, later broken up |
| 42 | M42 ONF | 1823514 | Scania L113CRL | Northern Counties Paladin | 4717 | B51F | 1994 | 11/94 | SMR |  |
| 43 | M113 RNK | 1823073 | Scania L113CRL | Northern Counties Paladin | 4714 | B49F | 1994 | 12/94 | SMR | Ex demonstrator |
| 10 | M210 NDB | 1823843 | Scania N113DRB | East Lancs | B12101 | H45/31F | 1995 | 2/95 | SMR |  |
| 11 | M211 NDB | 1823844 | Scania N113DRB | East Lancs | B12102 | H45/31F | 1995 | 2/95 | SMR |  |
|  | UWY 80X | 8030899 | Leyland Leopard PSU3F/4R | Duple Dominant IV Express | 134/5349 | C49F | 1981 | 4/95 | 6/95 | Ex Yorkshire Rider (1659) |
|  | VXI 8973 | 8030937 | Leyland Leopard PSU5C/4R | Plaxton Supreme IV | 8012LC046 | C50F | 1981 | 10/95 | 11/96 | Ex (MRJ 273W) Bluebird, Middleton (73) |
| 5/35 | MNC 487W | 7806339 | Leyland Fleetline FE30AGR | Northern Counties | 8905 | H43/32F | 1980 | 1/96 | 11/02 | Ex GMS Buses (4144). Became IAZ 4775 2/96. Not used summer 02. #35 9/02 |
| 6/36 | MNC 488W | 7806266 | Leyland Fleetline FE30AGR | Northern Counties | 8906 | H43/32F | 1980 | 1/96 | 11/02 | Ex GMS Buses (4145). Became IAZ 4776 2/96. Not used summer 01 & 02. #36 9/02 |
| 67 | N67 YVR | 1465 | Dennis Javelin 12SDA2155 | UVG Unistar | 5104/96 | C55F | 1996 | 2/96 | MC | Became BIG 4667 in 5/06 |
|  | JWA 27W | 8030180 | Leyland Leopard PSU3E/4R | Willowbrook | 802264 | C47F | 1981 | 2/96 | 11/96 | Ex Midland Red South (27) |
|  | BVP 791V | 7930061 | Leyland Leopard PSU3E/4R | Willowbrook | 79862 | C49F | 1980 | 2/96 | 2/96 | Ex Midland Red South (9) |
|  | ELJ 209V | 790243 | Leyland Leopard PSU3E/4R | Plaxton Supreme IV | 7911LX520 | C53F | 1979 | 2/96 | 2/96 | Ex Midland Red South (2026) |
| 68 | N68 YVR | 1466 | Dennis Javelin 12SDA2155 | UVG Unistar | 5105/96 | C55F | 1996 | 3/96 | MC | Became BIG 4668 in 6/06 |
| 36 | BVR 100T | 7804945 | Leyland Fleetline FE30AGR | Northern Counties | 8604 | H43/32F | 1979 | 9/96 | 7/01 | Ex GMS Buses (4100). In service: 9/96 |
| 37 | KDB 137V | 7805990 | Leyland Fleetline FE30AGR | Northern Counties | 8847 | H43/32F | 1980 | 9/96 | 7/01 | Ex GMS Buses (4137). In service: 9/96 |
| 56 | N56 CNF | 6063631 | Bova FLC12.290 XL9AA12NGT | Bova Futura Club |  | C55F | 1996 | 5/96 | MC | Became SIL 3856 in 2/00 |
| 61 | VRC 610Y | 8230901 | Leyland Leopard PSU3G/4R | Plaxton Supreme V Express | 8211LL5SX512 | C53F | 1982 | 9/96 | by 09? | Ex Trent (1610). In service: 9/96. Became LIL 9924 10/97 |
|  | BVR 68T | 7803948 | Leyland Fleetline FE30AGR | Northern Counties | 8572 | H43/32F | 1979 | 7/96 | 8/96 | Ex Barry Cooper. |

| Fleet No | Reg. No | Chassis | Number | Bodywork | Number | Capacity* | New | In | Out | Notes |
|---|---|---|---|---|---|---|---|---|---|---|
| 1 | P101 HNC | Scania N113DRB | 1827716 | East Lancs Cityzen | B17901 | H45/31F | 1996 | 8/96 | 3/04 | Intended as N101 DNA |
| 2 | P102 HNC | Scania N113DRB | 1827717 | East Lancs Cityzen | B17902 | H45/31F | 1996 | 8/96 | 3/04 | Intended as N102 DNA |
| 38 | SND 425X | Leyland Atlantean AN68B/1R | 8100966 | Northern Counties | 2136 | H43/32F | 1981 | 8/96 | 8/00 | Ex Stagecoach M/cr (4425). Became NIL 8258 on 12/9/97 |
| 39 | SND 484X | Leyland Atlantean AN68A/1R | 8101550 | Northern Counties | 2209 | H43/32F | 1982 | 8/96 | 8/99 | Ex Stagecoach M/cr (4484) |
| 3 | P103 HNC | Scania N113DRB | 1827914 | East Lancs Cityzen | B17903 | H45/31F | 1996 | 9/96 | 2/06 | |
| 4 | P104 HNC | Scania N113DRB | 1827915 | East Lancs Cityzen | B17904 | H45/31F | 1996 | 9/96 | ?/06 | |
| 40/59 | G509 SAP | Dennis Javelin 12SDA1928 | 542 | Duple 320 | 8980/1175 | C53F | 1990 | 10/96 | 4/97 | Ex Brighton & Hove (509) |
| 35 | SND 453X | Leyland Atlantean AN68A/1R | 8002905 | Northern Counties | 2170 | H43/32F | 1981 | 12/96 | 8/99 | Ex Stagecoach M/cr (4453) |
| 36 | SND 479X | Leyland Atlantean AN68A/1R | 8001784 | Northern Counties | 2204 | H43/32F | 1982 | 12/96 | 7/98 | Ex Stagecoach M/cr (4479) |
| 32 | SND 483X | Leyland Atlantean AN68B/1R | 8101879 | Northern Counties | 2208 | H43/32F | 1982 | 12/96 | 8/00 | Ex Stagecoach M/cr (4483) |
| 7 | SND 476X | Leyland Atlantean AN68B/1R | 8101204 | Northern Counties | 2201 | H43/32F | 1982 | 1/97 | 8/99 | Ex Stagecoach M/cr (4476) |
| 18 | SND 489X | Leyland Atlantean AN68B/1R | 8003058 | Northern Counties | 2214 | H43/32F | 1982 | 1/97 | 8/99 | Ex Stagecoach M/cr (4489) |
| 75 | P75 JND | Volvo B10M | YV31MA618VAO46304 | Plaxton Premiere 320 | 12VUN6038 | C55F | 1997 | 4/97 | 11/02 | del 2/4/97. Became TKU 540 in 10/01. Destroyed by fire |
| 76/78 | P76 JND | Volvo B10M | YV31MA618VAO46306 | Plaxton Premiere 320 | 12VUN6040 | C55F | 1997 | 3/97 | MC | del 21/2/97. Became EUK 978 in 03/00 & f/ no 78 in 12/02 |
| 71 | E644 DAU | DAF MB230LB615 | 299350 | Plaxton Paramount 3200II | 8812DVP3CO1N | C53F | 1988 | 5/97 | 5/04 | Ex Trent (1644). In service 6/97. RAZ 5171 9/97-4/04. Converted to C55F 5/98 |
| 72 | D634 WNU | DAF MB230DKFL615 | 289031 | Plaxton Paramount 3200II | 8712DVP3CO1N | C53F | 1987 | 5/97 | 9/00 | Ex Trent (1634). Became RAZ 5172 9/97 & C55F 10/97 |
| 8 | R108 YBA | Scania N113DRB | 1829343 | East Lancs Cityzen | B18501 | H45/33F | 1997 | 9/97 | SMR | |
| 9 | R109 YBA | Scania N113DRB | 1829344 | East Lancs Cityzen | B18502 | H45/33F | 1997 | 10/97 | SMR | |
| 24 | R24 YNC | Dennis Dart 9.8SFD412BR5STGD | 13423 | Marshall Dartline | C37 139 | B39F | 1997 | 9/97 | SMR | |
| 73 | D637 WNU | DAF MB230DKFL615 | 290223 | Plaxton Paramount 3200II | 8712DVP3C04N | C53F | 1987 | 11/97 | 7/02 | Ex Trent (1637). In service as NIL 9773 1/97. C55F by 5/98 |
| 74 | D643 WNU | DAF MB230DKFL615 | 294297 | Plaxton Paramount 3200II | 8712DVP3C09N | C53F | 1987 | 11/97 | 5/04 | Ex Trent (1643). In service as NIL 9774 3/98. C55F by 5/98 |
| 45 | R45 CNB | Dennis Dart SLF | 12004 | Marshall Capital | B171050 | B37F | 1998 | 3/98 | SMR | |
| 46 | R46 CNB | Dennis Dart SLF | 12007 | Marshall Capital | B171051 | B37F | 1998 | 3/98 | SMR | |
| 47 | R47 CNB | Dennis Dart SLF | 12009 | Marshall Capital | B171052 | B37F | 1998 | 3/98 | SMR | |
| 48 | R48 CNB | Denn s Dart SLF | 11994 | Marshall Capital | B171053 | B37F | 1998 | 3/98 | SMR | |
| 49 | R49 CNB | Dennis Dart SLF | 11995 | Marshall Capital | B171054 | B37F | 1998 | 3/98 | SMR | |
| 59/52 | D639 WNU | DAF MB230DKFL615 | 290714 | Plaxton Paramount 3200II | 8712DVP3C06N | C55F | 1987 | 3/98 | 7/02 | Ex Trent (1637) as C53F. Became PIL 7752 in 11/98 |
| 60/53 | D640 WNU | DAF MB230DKFL615 | 291601 | Plaxton Paramount 3200II | 8712DVP3C08N | C55F | 1987 | 3/98 | 9/00 | Ex Trent (1643) as C53F. In service 5/98. CLZ 8353 9/98 |
| 63 | S63 TNA | Scania L94 ib 4x2 | 1833095 | Irizar InterCentury | 150279 | C55F | 1998 | 9/98 | MC | del 11/9/98. TKU 540 12/02 |
| 57 | S57 TNA | Bova FHD12-340 | 7003501 | Bova Futura | | C49Ft | 1998 | 10/98 | MC | Became LIB 6437 in 12/02 |
| 64 | T64 JDB | Scania L94 ib 4x2 | 1833136 | Irizar InterCentury | 150272 | C55F | 1998 | 2/99 | MC | Became 403 BGO in 12/02 |
| 58 | T58 JDB | Bova FHD12-340 | 7003511 | Bova Futura | | C49Ft | 1998 | 3/99 | MC | Became NIL 8258 in 12/02 |
| 65/76 | T65 JDB | Scania L94 ib 4x2 | 1833137 | Irizar InterCentury | 150278 | C50Ft | 1998 | 4/99 | MC | IAZ 4776 & #76 from 12/02 |
| 60 | J247 MFP | Volvo B10M-60 | 24804 | Plaxton Paramount 3500IV | 9012VCB2047 | C46Ft | 1992 | 7/99 | MC | Ex Arriva. RIL 8160 10/99 |
| 25 | V125 DJA | Dennis Trident | 20458 | East Lancs Lowlyne | EL29004 | H51/31F | 1999 | 9/99 | SMR | |
| 26 | V126 DJA | Dennis Trident | 20432 | East Lancs Lowlyne | EL29002 | H51/31F | 1999 | 9/99 | SMR | |
| 27 | V127 DJA | Dennis Trident | 20448 | East Lancs Lowlyne | EL29003 | H51/31F | 1999 | 9/99 | SMR | |
| 28 | V128 DJA | Dennis Trident | 20459 | East Lancs Lowlyne | EL29005 | H51/31F | 1999 | 9/99 | SMR | |

| Fleet No | Reg. No | Chassis | Number | Bodywork | Number | Capacity* | New | In | Out | Notes |
|---|---|---|---|---|---|---|---|---|---|---|
| 29 | V129 DJA | Dennis Trident | 20431 | East Lancs Lowlyne | EL29001 | H51/31F | 1999 | 9/99 | SMR | |
| 81 | W81 JBN | Volvo B7R-63 | 000141 | Plaxton Prima | 9812VLM7791 | C55F | 2000 | 3/00 | MC | |
| 82 | W82 JBN | Volvo B7R-73 | 000161 | Plaxton Prima | 9912TCM1257 | C55F | 2000 | 3/00 | 5/04 | |
| 83 | W83 JBN | Volvo B7R-73 | 001431 | Plaxton Prima | 9912TCM1663 | C55F | 2000 | 4/00 | MC | |
| 18 | X118 YBA | Scania N113DRB | 1832996 | East Lancs Cityzen | 27604 | H47/31F | 2000 | 9/00 | 4/04 | |
| 19 | X119 YBA | Scania N113DRB | 1832997 | East Lancs Cityzen | 27605 | H47/31F | 2000 | 9/00 | 4/04 | |
| 20 | C110 UBC | Scania N112DRB | 1809026 | East Lancs | A6601 | H46/33F | 1986 | 4/01 | 5/02 | Ex Brighton & Hove (740) |
| 21 | C111 UBC | Scania N112DRB | 1809027 | East Lancs | A6602 | H46/33F | 1986 | 4/01 | 5/02 | Ex Brighton & Hove (741) |
| 22 | C112 UBC | Scania N112DRB | 1809028 | East Lancs | A6603 | H46/33F | 1986 | 4/01 | 5/02 | Ex Brighton & Hove (742) |
| 23 | C113 UBC | Scania N112DRB | 1809029 | East Lancs | A6604 | H46/33F | 1986 | 4/01 | 5/02 | Ex Brighton & Hove (743) |
| 20 | E701 EFG | Scania N112DRB | 1813189 | East Lancs | A8401 | H47/33F | 1988 | 4/02 | 4/04 | Ex Brighton & Hove (701) |
| | E703 EFG | Scania N112DRB | 1813191 | East Lancs | A8403 | H47/33F | 1988 | 5/02 | c12/03 | Ex Brighton & Hove (703) for parts. |
| 21 | E704 EFG | Scania N112DRB | 1813192 | East Lancs | A8404 | H47/33F | 1988 | 4/02 | 9/05 | Ex Brighton & Hove (704) |
| 22 | E705 EFG | Scania N112DRB | 1813440 | East Lancs | A8405 | H47/33F | 1988 | 4/02 | ?? | Ex Brighton & Hove (705) |
| 23 | E706 EFG | Scania N112DRB | 1813441 | East Lancs | A8406 | H47/33F | 1988 | 4/02 | SMR | Ex Brighton & Hove (706) |
| 7 | E707 EFG | Scania N112DRB | 1813648 | East Lancs | A8407 | H47/33F | 1988 | 5/02 | 2/03 | Ex Brighton & Hove (707) |
| 5 | E709 EFG | Scania N112DRB | 1813650 | East Lancs | A8409 | H47/33F | 1988 | 5/02 | MC | Ex Brighton & Hove (709) |
| 6 | F711 LFG | Scania N113DRB | 1815237 | East Lancs | A8412 | H47/33F | 1989 | 4/02 | ?? | Ex Brighton & Hove (711) |
| 51 | YS02 XDW | Scania K114B | 1842253 | Irizar Century | 150960 | C55F | 2002 | 7/02 | MC | Became RAZ 5171 in ?? |
| 52 | YS02 XDX | Scania K114B | 1842642 | Irizar Century | 150961 | C55F | 2002 | 7/02 | MC | Became NIL 9774 in ? |
| 30 | MX03 KZN | Dennis Trident | 32641 | Plaxton | 8150 | H47/31F | 2003 | 3/03 | SMR | |
| 31 | MX03 KZP | Dennis Trident | 32640 | Plaxton | 8151 | H47/31F | 2003 | 3/03 | SMR | |
| 53 | YN03 WRW | Scania K114B | 1844638 | Irizar Century | 151180 | C55F | 2003 | 5/03 | MC | Became HIG 3853 in ?? |
| | F713 LFG | Scania N113DRB | 1815239 | East Lancs | A8411 | H47/33F | 1989 | 7/03 | 4/04 | Ex Brighton & Hove (713) |
| | F715 LFG | Scania N113DRB | 1815241 | East Lancs | A8413 | H47/33F | 1989 | 7/03 | 7/03 | Ex Brighton & Hove (715) |
| 20 | F716 LFG | Scania N113DRB | 1815702 | East Lancs | A8420 | H47/33F | 1989 | 8/03 | SMR | Ex Brighton & Hove (716) |
| | F717 LFG | Scania N113DRB | 1815703 | East Lancs | A8416 | H47/33F | 1989 | 8/03 | 08/03 | Ex Brighton & Hove (717) |
| 40 | YN53 PCV | Scania N94UB | 1842133 | East Lancs | 44002 | B35F | 2003 | 1/04 | SMR | |
| 41 | YN53 GFJ | Scania N94UB | 1840362 | East Lancs | 44001 | B35F | 2004 | 1/04 | SMR | |
| 71 | L148 BFV | Dennis Javelin 11SDL2133 | 890 | Plaxton | 9311HZM1452 | C47F | 1993 | 3/04 | MC | Ex Sovereign (748). Became C49F and RAZ 5171 in 4/04 |
| 74 | L107 SDY | Dennis Javelin 11SDL2133 | 929 | Plaxton | 9311HZM1467 | C47F | 1994 | 3/04 | MC | Ex Sovereign (717). Became C49F & NIL 9774 in 4/04 |
| 75 | L102 SDY | Dennis Javelin 11SDL2133 | 923 | Plaxton | 9311HZM1463 | C47F | 1994 | 3/04 | MC | Ex Harrogate & Dist (166). Cvtd to C49F & IAZ 4775 4/04 |
| 18 | NDZ 3160 | Dennis Dart 85SDL3015 | 1359 | Wright Handybus | P325 | B29F | 1993 | 4/04 | SMR(z) | Ex Brighton & Hove (30). Withdrawn -/07 |
| 19 | NDZ 3161 | Dennis Dart 85SDL3015 | 1362 | Wright Handybus | P326 | B29F | 1993 | 4/04 | SMR | Ex Brighton & Hove (31) |
| 44 | K129 LGO | Dennis Dart 85SDL3015 | 1158 | Wright Handybus | P233 | B29F | 1992 | 4/04 | SMR | Ex Brighton & Hove (29). In service 3/05. |
| | E702 EFG | Scania N113DRB | 1813190 | East Lancs | A8402 | H47/33F | 1988 | 4/04 | 4/04 | Ex Brighton & Hove (702). To Scania, Worksop, direct |
| | E708 EFG | Scania N113DRB | 1813649 | East Lancs | A8408 | H47/33F | 1988 | 4/04 | 4/04 | Ex Brighton & Hove (708). To Scania, Worksop, direct |
| | E710 EFG | Scania N113DRB | 1813651 | East Lancs | A8410 | H47/33F | 1988 | 4/04 | 4/04 | Ex Brighton & Hove (710). To Scania, Worksop, direct |
| 59 | YN04 GPZ | Scania K124IB4 | 1847486 | Irizar | 101568 | C49Ft | 2004 | 6/04 | MC | |
| | F714 LFG | Scania N113DRB | 1815240 | East Lancs | A8414 | H47/33F | 1989 | 10/04 | 10/04 | Ex Brighton & Hove (714). To PC Coaches, Lincoln, direct |

| Fleet No | Reg. No | Chassis | Number | Bodywork | Number | Capacity* | New | In | Out | Notes |
|---|---|---|---|---|---|---|---|---|---|---|
|  | F718 LFG | Scania N113DRB | 1815704 | East Lancs | A8417 | H47/33F | 1989 | 10/04 | 10/04 | Ex Brighton & Hove (718) |
|  | F720 LFG | Scania N113DRB | 1815706 | East Lancs | A8418 | H47/33F | 1989 | 10/04 | 10/04 | Ex Brighton & Hove (720) |
|  | G722 RYG | Scania N113DRB | 1816947 | East Lancs | A8423 | H47/33F | 1990 | 10/04 | 10/04 | Ex Brighton & Hove (722) |
| 37 | M113 SLS | Scania L113CRL | 1824070 | Wright Access Ultralow | T45 | B47F | 1995 | 3/05 | SMR | Ex Nottingham (520) |
| 38 | M521 UTV | Scania L113CRL | 1824672 | Wright Access Ultralow | U63 | B51F | 1995 | 3/05 | SMR | Ex Nottingham (521) |
| 39 | M522 UTV | Scania L113CRL | 1824673 | Wright Access Ultralow | U64 | B51F | 1995 | 3/05 | SMR | Ex Nottingham (522) |
|  | BUI 1424 | Scania N112DRB | 1811346 | Van Hool | 13053 | C47F | 1987 | 2/06 | /08 | Ex Bullock, Cheadle (E213 FLD). For parts |
|  | FJ55 KMZ | Iveco | 150E24 | Vehixel Skolabus | 97024 | B67FL | 2005 | 11/05 | 12/05 | GMPTE Yellow School Bus. Re-allocated from Ace, Gorton |
| 36 | N632 XBU | Scania L113CRL | 1825896 | Wright Access Ultralow | U206 | B42F | 1995 | ?/07 | SMR | Ex TM Travel |

## Fleet History of Barry Cooper/Mayne Coaches, Warrington

| Fleet No | Reg. No | Chassis | Number | Bodywork | Number | Capacity* | New | In | Out | Notes |
|---|---|---|---|---|---|---|---|---|---|---|
|  | 636 RTJ | Commer Commercial |  |  |  | M12? | 1960 | c3/60 | ?? |  |
|  | SFR 295 | Ford 510E | 28511 | Burlingham | 6926 | C41F | 1960 | 10/63 | 5/64 | Ex Monks. Leigh |
|  | DTD 468B | Ford 676E | 836014 | Duple Marauder | 1174/8 | C52F | 1964 | 4/64 | 5/66 |  |
|  | 619 STB | Bedford SB1 | 85919 | Duple | 1133/125 | C41F | 1961 | 8/64 | by -/70 | Ex Monks. Leigh |
|  | 3854 DG | Bedford SB3 | 93279 | Duple Northern | 1170/28 | C41F | 1964 | 11/64 | 5/66 | Ex Talbot, Moreton |
|  | 134 EWW | Bedford VAL14 | 1129 | Plaxton Val | 632657 | C52F | 1963 | 12/64 | 6/65 | Ex Gray, Hoyland Common |
|  | CED 764C | Bedford VAL14 | 1851 | Plaxton Val | 653193 | C52F | 1965 | 7/65 | 12/68 | white, blue and red colours |
|  | DED 915C | Ford R226 | BC04ER16169 | Duple | 1204/3 | C52F | 1966 | 1/66 | 8/67 |  |
|  | MTJ 402C | Bedford SB5 | 95774 | Plaxton | 652643 | C41F | 1965 | 1/66 | 9/68 | Ex Walls, Wigan |
|  | GPW 443D | Bedford VAM5 | 1008 | Plaxton | 669114 | C45F | 1966 | 6/66 | 2/69 | Ex Carter, Northwold. Had 'Brazilian Football Team 1966' lettering on front |
|  | JED 181E | Bedford VAL14 | 7835687 | Plaxton Val | 672569 | C52F | 1967 | 7/67 | 3/71 |  |
|  | UTF 100D | Bedford VAL14 | 6818014 | Plaxton Val | 669384 | C52F | 1966 | 12/67 | 6/70 | Ex Tatlock, Whitefield |
|  | JVM 48OF | Ford Transit | BC05M07592 |  |  | M12 | 1968 | 2/68 | 3/69 |  |
|  | MED 732F | Bedford SB5 | 7T458430 | Plaxton | 689497 | C41F | 1968 | 8/68 | 9/72 |  |
|  | NED 537G | Bedford VAL70 | 459578 | Plaxton Panorama | 692403 | C53F | 1968 | 11/68 | 4/73 |  |
|  | LVR 267G | Ford Transit | BC05HS45290 |  |  | M12 | 1969 | 2/69 | 1/71 |  |
|  | OED 130G | Bedford SB5 | 7T459420 | Plaxton Panorama II | 692112 | C41F | 1969 | 2/69 | 5/73 |  |
|  | 631 UTD | Bedford SB1 | 86650 | Duple Bella Vista | 1133/211 | C41F | 1961 | 6/69 | 6/70 | Ex Kynaston, Newton |
|  | XRJ 193 | Bedford VAL14 | 1042 | Plaxton Val | 632554 | C52F | 1963 | 7/69 | 8/70 | Ex Mather, ? |
|  | KTB 100F | Bedford VAL70 | 7T450302 | Plaxton Panorama | 688591 | C52F | 1968 | 4/70 | 2/72 | Ex Tatlock, Whitefield |
|  | SED 562H | Bedford VAL70 | 9T471050 | Plaxton Panorama | 708358 | C53F | 1970 | 4/70 | 4/74 |  |
|  | ANJ 57B | Ford 570E | L80C837699 | Duple | 1173/43 | C41F | 1964 | 6/70 | 7/71 |  |
|  | PVR 332J | Ford Transit | BC05KA43858 |  |  | M12 | 1971 | 1/71 | 1/72 |  |
|  | LTF 224C | Bedford VAS1 | 1904 | Duple Bella Vista | 1184/4 | C29F | 1965 | 6/71 | 5/72 | Ex Kynaston, Newton |
|  | VED 598J | Bedford VAL70 | 1T483335 | Plaxton Panorama IV | 712419 | C53F | 1971 | 7/71 | 3/75 |  |
|  | VED 895J | Bedford SB5 | 1T483184 | Plaxton | 712158 | C41F | 1971 | 7/71 | 7/75 |  |
|  | KDJ 999 | AEC Regent V | 2D3RA746 | East Lancs | 5615 | H41/32F | 1959 | 10/71 | 8/72 | Ex Conroy, St Albans |
|  | YED 779K | Bedford VAL70 | 2T471971 | Plaxton Panorama | 728378 | C53F | 1972 | 3/72 | 1/77 |  |
|  | YED 780K | Bedford VAS5 | 2T471671 | Plaxton | 728084 | C29F | 1972 | 3/72 | 4/76 |  |
|  | AED 673X | Bedford SB5 | 2T472708 | Plaxton | 728130 | C41F | 1972 | 6/72 | 7/74 |  |
|  | KCN 184 | Leyland PDR1/1 | 591511 | Alexander | 5922 | H44/34F | 1960 | 10/72 | 3/74 | Ex Gateshead & District |
|  | DED 443L | Bedford SB5 | 2T476904 | Plaxton | 732089 | C41F | 1973 | 2/73 | 1/77 |  |
|  | GBU 462D | Bedford VAL14 | 6819254 | Duple Vega | 1202/65 | C52F | 1966 | 2/73 | 4/73 | Ex Stott, Oldham |

| Fleet No | Reg. No | Chassis | Number | Bodywork | Number | Capacity* | New | In | Out | Notes |
|---|---|---|---|---|---|---|---|---|---|---|
|  | EED 705L | Bedford YRT | 2T476569 | Duple Dominant | 272/170 | C53F | 1973 | 3/73 | 10/76 | Withdrawn 3/76 |
|  | NED 293M | Bedford YRT | CW457815 | Plaxton Panorama II | 732746 | C53F | 1973 | 9/73 | 8/76 |  |
|  | TTJ 845D | Bedford VAL14 | 6825351 | Plaxton Val | 669396 | C52F | 1966 | 9/73 | 8/74 | Ex Bellairs & Dootson, Leigh |
|  | MEL 988F | Bedford VAL70 | 1T451017 | Duple | 182/53 | C52F | 1968 | 1/74 | 8/75 | Ex Shamrock & Rambler |
|  | VEN 415L | Bedford SB5 | CW453796 | Plaxton Panorama | 732120 | C41F | 1973 | 4/74 | 9/76 | Ex Byng, Portsmouth |
|  | LBU 140L | Bedford YRT | 2T477343 | Plaxton | 732375 | C53F | 1973 | 5/74 | 6/77 | Ex Byng, Portsmouth. Withdrawn 3/76 |
|  | WRM 92H | Bedford VAL70 | 0T475600 | Plaxton VAL | 708399 | C53F | 1970 | 12/74 | 5/78 | Ex Kinsey, Chester. Wdn 7/76 |
|  | UEB 464K | Leyland Leopard PSU3B/4RT | 7101592 | Plaxton Panorama Elite II | 719034 | C51F | 1972 | 1/75 | 4/83 | Ex Harris, Cambridge |
| 11 | SCK 869 | Leyland Leopard PSU3/3RT | 621513 | Plaxton Panorama Elite III (7/76) | 7611LC059S | C49F | 1962 | 5/75 | 2/90 | Ex PMT (19) with Duple C40Ft body. Became C53F in 7/85 & ACA 642A in 11/86 |
|  | HDJ 650N | AEC Reliance | 6U3ZR29581 | Plaxton Panorama Elite III | 7511AC001 | C53F | 1975 | 8/75 | 10/80 | Naylors of Cheshire titles |
|  | JED 60N | Leyland Leopard PSU3/3RT | 621512 | Plaxton Panorama Elite III (8/75) | 7511LC29S | C53F | 1962 | 8/75 | 6/79 | Ex Ribble/PMT and originally Duple C40Ft, SCK 878 |
|  | JTB 868P | Bedford SB5 | EW455741 | Plaxton Panorama Elite III | 75NJM001 | C41F | 1975 | 8/75 | 11/78 |  |
| 7 | JTB 869P | Leyland Leopard PSU5A/4R | 7503028 | Plaxton Panorama Elite III | 7512LC004 | C57F | 1975 | 9/75 | 2/87 | Became 480 XYB in 01/87 |
|  | KEK 3P | Leyland Leopard PSU3/3RT | 620003 | Plaxton Panorama Elite III (8/75) | 7511LC030S | C53F | 1962 | 9/75 | 2/80 | Ex PMT (917), as 917 UVT |
|  | TCK 716 | Leyland Leopard PSU3/3RT | L00327 | Harrington |  | C49F | 1963 | 9/75 | 5/77 | Ex Jones, Aberbeeg |
|  | PND 998J | Austin Morris 250JU | 31067 | BLMC |  | M12 | 1971 | c-/76 | 10/76 | Ex Corley, Hazel Grove |
|  | MEK 212P | Leyland Leopard PSU3C/4R | 7600877 | Plaxton Supreme III | 7611LC072 | C53F | 1976 | 3/76 | 5/85 | Ex Tatlock, Whitefield |
|  | LJP 398P | Leyland Leopard PSU3/3RT | L00329 | Plaxton (rebody 2/76) | 7511LC046SM | C53F | 1963 | 3/76 | 1/82 | Ex PMT, originally new to Ribble as TCK 720 with Harrington C49F body |
|  | KLR 458D | Leyland Leopard PSU3/3RT | L60864 | Duple | 169/5 | C49F | 1966 | 3/76 | 10/79 | Ex National Travel South East |
|  | NMX 583E | AEC Reliance | 6MU4R6567 | Plaxton Panorama | 672981 | C41F | 1967 | 3/76 | 1/77 | Ex National Travel South East |
|  | TA0 397 | AEC Reliance | MU3RV1142 | Plaxton (rebody 2/71) | 712891 | C45F | 1957 | 8/76 | 10/76 | Ex Caven, Bury and originally had a Plaxton C41C body |
|  | GBU 30K | AEC Reliance | MU3RA1946 | Plaxton (rebody) | 728789 | C41F | 1972 | 8/76 | 7/77 |  |
|  | ODJ 51R | Leyland Leopard PSU3C/4R | 7601386 | Plaxton Supreme III | 7611LC077 | C53F | 1976 | 8/76 | 5/85 |  |
|  | ODJ 52R | Bedford SB5 | FW454156 | Plaxton Supreme III | 76NJM003 | C41F | 1976 | 8/76 | 6/82 |  |
|  | SGF 484L | Bristol RELH6L | RELH-4/269 | Duple |  | C51F | 1973 | 1/77 | 8/77 | Ex National Travel South East. Withdrawn 7/77 |
|  | PJP 274R | Bedford SB5 | FW458727 | Plaxton Supreme III | 77NJM001 | C41F | 1977 | 1/77 | 4/82 |  |
|  | PJP 275R | Leyland Leopard PSU3/4R | BC2/77 (629752) | Plaxton Supreme III (2/77) | 7711LC067/S | C53F | 1963 | 3/77 | 5/86 | Ex Davies, Halewood. Originally 91 FXD with Park Royal C49F body |
|  | PJP 276R | Leyland Leopard LT2 | BC1/77 (602624) | Plaxton Supreme III (3/77) | 7710LCM001S | C45F | 1961 | 4/77 | 5/86 | Ex Chorlton High School. New to Northern General as MCN 56, with Harrington C37F body |
|  | HDG 362D | Leyland Leopard PSU3/3R | L62068 | Plaxton | 669808 | C47F | 1966 | 7/77 | 6/79 | Ex National Travel South West |
|  | HDG 363D | Leyland Leopard PSU3/3R | L62067 | Plaxton | 669809 | C47F | 1966 | 7/77 | 1/79 | Ex National Travel South West. Naylors colours |
|  | CHA 115C | Leyland Leopard PSU3/4R | L42123 | Duple | 163/42 | C49F | 1965 | 8/77 | 4/79 | Ex National Travel South West |
|  | CHA 118C | Leyland Leopard PSU3/4R | L42124 | Duple | 163/45 | C49F | 1965 | 8/77 | 12/79 | Ex National Travel South West |
|  | SFM 998R | Bedford YMT | FW455075 | Plaxton | 7611TC097 | C53F | 1976 | 10/77 | 12/78 | Ex Naylor, Stockton Heath |
|  | UTB 542S | Leyland Leopard PSU3E/4R | 7608379 | Plaxton Viewmaster | 7711LCV083 | C53F | 1978 | 3/78 | 3/87? | Naylors fleet names (until 82) |
|  | BUN 457L | Leyland Leopard PSU3B/4R | 7300006 | Plaxton Panorama Elite III | 733783 | C53F | 1973 | 4/78 | 12/83 | Ex Hamner, Southsea |
| 14 | VJP 391S | Leyland Leopard LT2 | BC3/78 (602646) | Plaxton Supreme III (4/78) | 7810LCMS001 | C45F | 1961 | 4/78 | ?/89 | New to Northern General as MCN 61, with Harrington C37F body |
|  | AED 132T | Leyland Leopard PSU5B/4R | 7801661 | Plaxton Viewmaster | 7812LCM046 | C57F | 1978 | 8/78 | 11/83 |  |

| Fleet No | Reg. No | Chassis | Number | Bodywork | Number | Capacity* | New | In | Out | Notes |
|---|---|---|---|---|---|---|---|---|---|---|
|  | DUR 973K | Leyland Leopard PSU3B/4R | 7102114 | Duple | 242/9 | C51F | 1972 | 10/78 | 5/80 | Ex Best, London W5 |
|  | TGD 992R | Volvo B58-56 | 7665 | Plaxton Viewmaster | 7711VCV002 | C53F | 1977 | 12/78 | 3/84 | Ex Parks, Hamilton |
| 13 | BJP 642T | Leyland Leopard PSU4/4R | BC4/79 (L60234) | Plaxton Supreme IV (4/79) | 7910LC006/S | C45F | 1966 | 4/79 | 3/90 | Ex Hants & Dorset. New to North Western as FJA 227D with Duple C41F body |
|  | DED 571T | Leyland Leopard PSU5C/4R | 7900462 | Plaxton Supreme IV | 7912LC086 | C57F | 1979 | 7/79 | 6/85 |  |
|  | FUB 479K | Leyland Leopard PSU3B/4R | 7200295 | Duple | 242/14 | C53F | 1972 | 7/79 | by 7/81 | Ex Crowther, Morley |
|  | EFM 96S | Leyland Leopard PSU3/4R | 7200295 | Plaxton Supreme III (rebody) | 7811LC068/S | C51F | 1964 | 9/79 | 5/86 | Ex Yates, Runcorn. Previously AAD 242B. Cream and black |
|  | KCK 982H | Leyland Leopard PSU4A/4R | 903700 | Plaxton | 709058 | C40F | 1970 | 2/80 | 3/81 | Ex National Travel South West |
| 12 | XND 4L | Leyland Leopard PSU5C/4R | 7300438 | Plaxton Panorama Elite III | 733135 | C57F | 1973 | 3/80 | 5/87 | Ex Finglands, Rusholme. Became 974 EYB by 9/86 |
|  | SHA 650G | Leyland Leopard PSU4A/4R | 900453 | Plaxton | 693171 | C43F | 1969 | 3/80 | 3/81 | Ex National Travel South West |
|  | JEK 121V | Volvo B58-61 | 14292 | Plaxton Viewmaster IV | 8012VCV917 | C57F | 1980 | 3/80 | 5/83 |  |
|  | TBO 3N | Volvo B58-56 | 5112 | Plaxton Elite Express III | 7411VX510 | C53F | 1974 | 11/80 | 2/82 | Ex Gardiner, Spennymoor |
| 17 | ODJ 417W | Leyland Leopard PSU5D/4R | 7905022 | Plaxton Supreme IV | 8112LC034 | C57F | 1981 | 3/81 | c11/96 | Became VGU 443 in 12/82 |
|  | OJP 908W | Leyland Leopard PSU3A/4R | BC5/81 (7002603) | Duple Dominant III (3/81) | 133/5174 | C53F | 1970 | 4/81 | 11/83 | Ex Midland Red North, WHA 252H with Plaxton C49F body |
|  | DFM 881X | Leyland Leopard PSU3A/4R | BC6/81 (7001281) | Duple Dominant III (8/81) | 133/5175 | C53F | 1970 | 4/81 | 5/84 | Ex Midland Red North, WHA 229H with Plaxton C49F body |
|  | TKW 723S | Volvo B58-61 | 9482 | Plaxton Viewmaster | 7812VCV003 | C53F | 1978 | 10/81 | 10/83 | Ex Littlewood, Sheffield |
| (r) | GDM 996X | Leyland Leopard PSU5/4R | BC7/81 (7003794) | Duple Dominant III (4/82) | 235/5436 | C57F | 1971 | ?/81 | 4/82 | Originally VUR 217J with Van Hool Vistadome C53F body. Rebuilt and sold to PG Travel, Middlewich |
| 10 | PTO 350R | Leyland Leopard PSU5A/4R | 7602942 | Plaxton Supreme III | 7612LC035AM | C57F | 1976 | 5/83 | ?/91 | Ex Mayne, Manchester. Became UCE 665 in 11/85. |
| 18/15 | A418 HND | Leyland Tiger TRCTL11/3R | 8201496 | Plaxton Paramount 3200 | 8312LTP1C077 | C57F | 1983 | 8/83 | 3/00 | Became YPL 764 in 11/85 & A533 XLG 3/00 |
| 19 | A419 HND | Leyland Tiger TRCTL11/3R | 8300357 | Duple Laser | 335/5335 | C57F | 1983 | 9/83 | 9/97 | Became YUC 765 in 11/85. |
| 23 | A423 LRJ | Leyland Tiger TRCTL11/3R | 8201007 | Plaxton Paramount 3200 | 8311LTP1X528 | C53F | 1984 | 1/84 | ?/91 | Became 614 BWU in 11/85, then A633 XFM |
| 22 | A422 KBA | Bedford PJK | ET101206 | Plaxton Supreme IV | 848PJS4CC001 | C29F | 1984 | 2/84 | 11/90 | Became UCE 665 in 05/90, then A609 XFM in 10/90. |
| 20 | A420 HND | Leyland Tiger TRCTL11/3R | 8201330 | Plaxton Paramount 3500 | 8312LTH1C04N | C57F | 1984 | 4/84 | 1/87 | 507 EXA 3/86. Part-ex for Trent Leopards 1/87 |
| 21/14 | A421 KBA | Leyland Tiger TRCTL11/3R | 8300197 | Plaxton Paramount 3500 | 8312LTH1C05N | C53Ft | 1984 | 4/84 | ?/97? | Became EUK 978 in 03/86 & A537 XLG in 03/00 |
|  | OUC 35R | Leyland Fleetline FE30AGR | 7601787 | Metro Cammell Weymann |  | H45/32F | 1976 | 1/85 | 3/85 | Ex Happy Days, Woodseaves. |
| 24/16 | B424 RNA | Leyland Tiger TRCTL11/3R | 8400298 | Plaxton Paramount 3200II | 8412LTP1C046 | C53F | 1985 | 3/85 | 1/03 | Became OED 201 in 11/85 & back to B424 RNA in 12/02 |
| 25/17 | B425 RNA | Leyland Tiger TRCTL11/3R | 8400332 | Plaxton Paramount 3200II | 8412LTP1C047 | C57F | 1985 | 3/85 | 3/00 | Became UOL 337 in 11/85 & B224 FMB in 02/00 |
| 16 | HDB 356V | Leyland Leopard PSU5C/4R | 7904773 | Plaxton Supreme IV | 8012LC071 | C57F | 1980 | 7/85 | 9/99 | Ex Mayne, Manchester. Became 289 BUA in 11/85 & UTU 673V in 9/99 |
| 15 | HDB 357V | Leyland Leopard PSU5C/4R | 7904950 | Plaxton Supreme IV | 8012LC072 | C57F | 1980 | 7/85 | c11/99 | Ex Mayne, Manchester. Became 906 GAU from 11/85 until 10/99 |
|  | ORO 325L | Leyland Leopard PSU5/4R | 7102233 | Van Hool Vistadome | 4032 | C57F | 1973 | 7/85 | 9/86 | Ex Pedley, Norton Canes |
| 66 | SNC 366X | Leyland Leopard PSU3A/5R | MM8101 (7001708) | Plaxton Supreme IV (4/82) | 8111LC054S | C53F | 1970 | 3/86 | 11/09 | Originally WHA 236H with Plaxton C49F body and rebuilt by Mayne, Manchester. Became UCE 665 in 10/91. Tow-bar in boot |
| 26 | C426 YBA | Leyland Tiger TRCTLXCT/3RZ | 8401183 | Plaxton Paramount 3500II | 8512LGH2C753 | C51F | 1986 | 3/86 | 1/99 | Became LIB 6440 in 10/88. |

| Fleet No | Reg. No | Chassis | Number | Bodywork | Number | Capacity* | New | In | Out | Notes |
|---|---|---|---|---|---|---|---|---|---|---|
| 11 | UTU 23V | Leyland Tiger TRCTL11/2R Sp | 7905555 | Duple Dominant II | 033/5199 | C49F | 1980 | 3/86 | ?/92 | Leyland test rig, first reg'd 9/86. SCK 869 from 11/86 |
| 54 | LJX 139 | Leyland Leopard PSU3F/5R | 7903768 | Plaxton Supreme IV | 8011LC015 | C53F | 1980 | 4/86 | 8/93 | Ex Mayne, HDB 354V. |
|  | - | Leyland Titan TNLX-/-/-- | 7501705 B15 01 (or 03) | Park Royal | B60766 (or B60768) | H-/-/-F | 1975 | ?/86 | ?/86 | Prototype acquired for parts. |
|  | XBF 59S | Leyland Leopard PSU3E/4R | 7705303 | Duple Dominant I Express | 834/5282 | C49F | 1978 | 1/87 | 3/87 | Ex PMT (59) |
|  | XBF 62S | Leyland Leopard PSU3E/4R | 7705093 | Duple Dominant I Express | 834/5212 | C49F | 1978 | 1/87 | ?/87 | Ex PMT (62). Not used |
|  | XBF 63S | Leyland Leopard PSU3E/4R | 7705114 | Duple Dominant I Express | 834/5211 | C49F | 1978 | 1/87 | ?/87 | Ex PMT (63). Not used |
|  | GRF 265V | Leyland Leopard PSU3E/4R | 7901971 | Duple Dominant II Express | 934/5321 | C53F | 1979 | 1/87 | 1/89 | Ex PMT (65) |
|  | GRF 267V | Leyland Leopard PSU3E/4R | 7902118 | Duple Dominant II Express | 934/5323 | C53F | 1979 | 1/87 | 1/90 | Ex PMT (67). Loaned to Mayne 5-12/87 & 10/88-3/89 |
|  | GRF 268V | Leyland Leopard PSU3E/4R | 7901978 | Duple Dominant II Express | 934/5324 | C53F | 1979 | 1/87 | ?/87 | Ex PMT (68) |
| 3 | SCP 343L | Leyland Leopard PSU4B/2R | 7202390 | Plaxton Derwent | 729921 | B45F | 1973 | 3/87 | 1/88 | Ex West Yorkshire (3003) |
| 4 | SCP 344L | Leyland Leopard PSU4B/2R | 7202391 | Plaxton Derwent | 729914 | B45F | 1973 | 3/87 | 1/88 | Ex West Yorkshire (3004) |
| 5 | SCP 345L | Leyland Leopard PSU4B/2R | 7202392 | Plaxton Derwent | 729920 | B45F | 1973 | 3/87 | 11/87 | Ex West Yorkshire (3005) |
| 55/63 | GWY 691N | Leyland Leopard PSU4B/2R | 7404641 | Plaxton Derwent | 7410LB802S | DP43F | 1975 | 3/87 | 10/87 | Ex West Yorkshire (3011). |
| 2 | NMX 643 | Leyland Leopard PSU3F/5R | 7903781 | Plaxton Supreme IV | 8011LC016 | C53F | 1980 | 8/87 | ?/07 | Ex Mayne, HDB 355V |
|  | SCP 342L | Leyland Leopard PSU4B/2R | 7202389 | Plaxton Derwent | 729922 | B45F | 1973 | 10/87 | 1/88 | Ex Mayne, Manchester |
|  | VUB 400H | Leyland Leopard PSU3A/4R | 7000938 | Plaxton Panorama Elite | 709189 | C53F | 1970 | 12/87 | 2/88 | Ex Stoniers, Tunstall for parts |
|  | PLG 503L | Bedford YRQ | 2T476995 | Duple Dominant | 266/102 | C45F | 1973 | 1/88 | 3/88 | From Lymmville |
|  | PLG 367P | Bedford YRQ | EW450710 | Duple Dominant | 615/2000 | C45F | 1976 | 1/88 | 1/90 | From Lymmville |
|  | FCW 808S | Bedford YMT | GW456085 | Duple Dominant II | 817/2430 | C53F | 1978 | 1/88 | 1/90 | From Lymmville |
|  | CAL 584T | Bedford YMT | HW453832 | Duple Dominant II | 917/2423 | C53F | 1979 | 1/88 | 3/88 | From Lymmville |
|  | FEK 187V | Bedford YRQ | JW452288 | Duple Dominant II | 915/2152 | C53F | 1980 | 1/88 | 4/89 | From Lymmville |
|  | EHB 259G | Leyland Leopard PSU4A/2R | 802729 | East Lancs | 6687 | B43F | 1969 | 2/88 | 4/96 | Ex Stonier, Goldenhill |
|  | ODM 500V | Leyland Leopard PSU3E/4R | 7901119 | Duple Dominant II Express | 934/5347 | C49F | 1979 | 3/88 | 6/90 | Ex Crosville (ELL500) |
| 6 | UJX 916M | Leyland Leopard PSU4B/2R | 7302898 | Plaxton Derwent | 733995 | B45F | 1973 | 4/88 | ?/90 | Ex Mayne, Manchester |
| 27 | F27 HNC | DAF SB2305DHTD585 | 309894 | Duple 320 | 8882/0779 | C57F | 1989 | 1/89 | 1/97 | Became 614 BWU 11/90 |
| 7 | JWU 252N | Leyland Leopard PSU4C/4R | 7501320 | Plaxton Derwent | 7510LB808 | B43F | 1975 | 1/89 | 4/90 | Ex Mayne, Manchester |
|  | MWW 563P | Leyland Leopard PSU3C/4R | 7505440 | Plaxton Supreme Express | 7611LX509 | C49F | 1976 | 2/89 | 10/91 | Ex West Yorkshire (2547). Became UCE 665 10/90 & RMA 734P 10/91 |
| 12 | RKH 312T | Leyland Leopard PSU3E/4R | 7900293 | Plaxton Supreme IV | 7911LC042 | C49F | 1979 | 4/89 | 10/93 | Ex Scarborough & District (195, FAG195T), as 165 DKH |
|  | C520 WBF | Leyland Tiger TRCTL11/3RZ | 8500801 | Duple 340 | 8395/0047 | C50Ft | 1986 | 2/90 | 9/94 | Ex Mayne, Manchester , becoming FIL 9386 in 02/90 |
|  | OVC 958P | Leyland Leopard PSU3C/4R | 7504915 | Plaxton Supreme Express | 7611LX561 | C49F | 1976 | 5/90 | 10/91 | Ex Midland Red South (68). Was JOX 454P, then 491 GAC |
| 51 | A351 KBA | Bedford PJK | ET100997 | Plaxton Supreme IV | 848PJS4C002 | C29F | 1984 | 11/90 | 3/93 | Ex Mayne, Manchester. Became CSU 918 in 09/91 |
|  | LIW 1324 | Leyland Leopard PSU3C/2R | 7603822 | Willowbrook | 76496 | B51F | 1976 | 2/91 | ?/92 | Ex Mayne (NTX 361R) |
| 61 | NIB 3261 | Leyland Leopard PSU5C/4R | 7930137 | Plaxton Supreme IV | 8112LC072 | C57F | 1981 | 2/91 | 10/01 | Ex Mayne (SNC 361X) |
|  | NTX 363R | Leyland Leopard PSU3C/2R | 7604168 | Willowbrook | 76498 | B51F | 1976 | 3/91 | ?/92 | Ex Mayne, Manchester |
| 28 | H28 FVM | Dennis Javelin 11SDL1921 | 1921/524 | Duple 320 | 8980/1159 | C55F | 1991 | 4/91 | 12/98 | Became XIB 3922 in 06/97 |
|  | NHL 201R | Leyland Leopard PSU5A/4R | 7602475 | Duple Dominant | 635/5221 | C57F | 1977 | 8/91 | 11/94 | Ex Progress, Denton. Became DIL 6907 by 9/92 |
| 29 | J29 LJA | Dennis Javelin 11SDL | 1921/521 | Duple 320 | 8978/1155 | C55F | 1991 | 8/91 | 12/98 |  |
| 10 | KUC 969P | Leyland Fleetline FE30AGR | 7600200 | Metro Cammell Weymann |  | H45/32F | 1976 | 1/94 | 3/94 | Loaned from Mayne, M/cr |
| 1 | OJD 131R | Leyland Fleetline FE30AGR | 7600796 | Park Royal | B60910 | H44/29F | 1977 | 1/94 | 3/99 | Withdrawn 10/98 |

| Fleet No | Reg. No | Chassis | Number | Bodywork | Number | Capacity* | New | In | Out | Notes |
|---|---|---|---|---|---|---|---|---|---|---|
|  | WPD 28Y | Leyland Leopard PSU3G/4R | 8230185 | Eastern Coach Works | 23551 | C49F | 1982 | 3/94 | 11/94 | Ex Alder Valley (1128) |
| 2 | KUC 969P | Leyland Fleetline FE30AGR | 7600200 | Metro Cammell Weymann |  | H45/32F | 1976 | 7/94 | 11/97 | Ex Mayne. Gardner engine |
| 4 | GND 505N | Daimler Fleetline CRG6LXB | 65952 | Northern Counties | 7719 | H43/32F | 1974 | 8/94 | 3/05 | Ex Mayne, Manchester. Withdrawn c11/02 |
| 8 | YNA 328M | Daimler Fleetline CRG6LXB | 65898 | Northern Counties | 7653 | H43/32F | 1973 | 9/94 | 9/97 | Ex Mayne, Manchester |
|  | ARB 134T | Leyland Leopard PSU3E/4R | 7802231 | Plaxton Supreme Express | 7811LXM527 | C49F | 1978 | 9/94 | c2/00 | Ex Mayne, Manchester |
|  | BRC 140T | Leyland Leopard PSU3E/4R | 7806414 | Plaxton Supreme Express | 7811LXM533 | C49F | 1979 | 9/94 | c2/00 | Ex Mayne, Manchester |
|  | SCH 149X | Leyland Leopard PSU3F/4R | 8030415 | Willowbrook 003 | 802405 | C49F | 1982 | 9/94 | 3/97 | Ex Mayne, Manchester |
|  | PCW 680P | Leyland Leopard PSU3C/4R | 7600169 | Duple Dominant Express | 634/5166 | C53F | 1976 | 12/94 | 8/97 | Ex Whitecross, Warrington. Became LIW 1322 1/96 |
|  | KVO 142W | Leyland Leopard PSU3E/4R | 7930161 | Willowbrook 003 | 79897 | C49F | 1981 | 1/95 | c1/97 | Ex Mayne, Manchester |
| 6 | ULS 666T | Leyland Fleetline FE30AGR | 7806432 | Eastern Coach Works | 23594 | H43/32F | 1979 | 8/95 | c12/02 | Ex Mayne, Manchester. Withdrawn 7/00 |
|  | ELJ 209V | Leyland Leopard PSU3E/4R | 790243 | Plaxton Supreme IV | 7911LX520 | C53F | 1979 | 2/96 | 6/96 | Ex Midland Red South (2026). For parts |
| 3 | ULS 663T | Leyland Fleetline FE30AGR | 7806355 | Eastern Coach Works | 23583 | H43/32F | 1979 | 4/96 | c12/02 | Ex Mayne. Withdrawn 7/00 |
|  | BVR 100T | Leyland Fleetline FE30AGR | 7804945 | Northern Counties | 8604 | H43/32F | 1979 | 4/96 | 6/96 | On loan from Mayne |
|  | KDB 137V | Leyland Fleetline FE30AGR | 7805990 | Northern Counties | 8847 | H43/32F | 1980 | 4/96 | 6/96 | On loan from Mayne |
|  | ANA 24T | Leyland Fleetline FE30AGR | 7801003 | Northern Counties | 8653 | H43/32F | 1978 | 4/96 | 6/96 | Ex GMS Buses (4024). Spares |
|  | BVR 68T | Leyland Fleetline FE30AGR | 7803948 | Northern Counties | 8572 | H43/32F | 1979 | 4/96 | 6/96 | Ex GMS Buses (4068) for Mayne, Manchester |
|  | XBU 2S | Leyland Fleetline FE30AGR | 7000729 | Northern Counties | 8631 | H43/32F | 1978 | 4/96 | 6/96 | Ex GMS Buses (4002). Spares |
|  | ANA 21T | Leyland Fleetline FE30AGR | 7801780 | Northern Counties | 8650 | H43/32F | 1978 | 4/96 | 6/96 | Ex GMS Buses (4021). Spares |
| 5 | OJD 163R | Leyland Fleetline FE30AGR | 7602788 | Park Royal | B60942 | H44/29F | 1976 | 8/96 | 6/01 | Ex Mayne, Manchester |
| 7 | THX 555S | Leyland Fleetline FE30ALR Sp | 7703261 | Park Royal | 61154 | H44/31F | 1978 | 8/96 | 2/06 | Ex Mayne, Manchester |
| | THX 322S | Leyland Fleetline FE30ALR Sp | 7702626 | Metro Cammell Weymann |  | H44/31F | 1978 | 3/97 | 4/97 | Ex Mayne. For parts |
| 65 | MJI 5765 | Leyland Leopard PSU5C/4R | 8030044 | Plaxton Supreme IV | 8112LC075 | C57F | 1982 | 3/97 | ?/07 | Ex Mayne (SNC 365X) |
| 21 | P121 JNF | Volvo B10M | YV31MA618VAO46234 | Plaxton Premiere 320 | 12VUN6017 | C55F | 1997 | 4/97 | c7/15 | del 3/97. 906 GAU 10/99 |
| 22 | P122 JNF | Volvo B10M | YV31MA618VAO46235 | Plaxton Premiere 320 | 12VUN6018 | C55F | 1997 | 5/97 | by 10/19 | 289 BUA 9/99. Later C57F |
| 23 | LIW 1323 | Leyland Leopard PSU3B/4R | 7304951 | Willowbrook Warrior (12/90) | 90050 | B48F | 1973 | 7/97 | 8/97 | Ex Mayne, Manchester |
| 9 | THX 303S | Leyland Fleetline FE30ALR Sp | 7702409 | Metro Cammell Weymann |  | H44/31F | 1978 | 7/97 | 8/02 | Ex Mayne, Manchester |
| 2 | TET 747S | Leyland Fleetline FE30AGR | 7608102 | Roe | G07899 | H43/33F | 1977 | 9/97 | c12/02 | Ex Stotts, Oldham. In service 11/97 & withdrawn 2/00 |
|  | TET 746S | Leyland Fleetline FE30AGR | 768101 | Roe | G07898 | H43/33F | 1977 | 9/97 | ?/02 | Ex Stotts, Oldham |
| 64 | MJI 5764 | Leyland Leopard PSU5C/4R | 8030035 | Plaxton Supreme IV | 8112LC074 | C57F | 1981 | 10/97 | 1/02 | Ex Mayne (SNC 364X) |
| 19 | R119 CNE | Volvo B10M-62 | 042244 | Plaxton Premiere 320 | 9712VUM6758 | C57F | 1998 | 2/98 | 8/11 | Became UOL 337 in 2/00 |
| 20 | R120 CNE | Volvo B10M-62 | 047326 | Plaxton Premiere 320 | 9712VUM7070 | C57F | 1998 | 2/98 | 8/11 | Became YPL 764 in 3/00 |
| 10 | THX 601S | Leyland Fleetline FE30ALR Sp | 7703767 | Park Royal | 61200 | H44/31F | 1978 | 3/98 | 12/02 | Ex Mayne, Manchester (31) |
| 11 | THX 594S | Leyland Fleetline FE30ALR Sp | 7704839 | Park Royal | 61193 | H44/31F | 1978 | 3/98 | 3/01 | Ex Mayne, Manchester (34) |
| 60 | GIL 2160 | Leyland Leopard PSU5C/4R | 8030050 | Plaxton Supreme IV | 8112LC067 | C57F | 1981 | 5/98 | 1/00 | Ex Mayne (MRJ 360W) |
| 23 | T223 JND | Scania L94 ib 4x2 | 1833716 | Irizar InterCentury | 150319 | C55F | 1999 | 5/99 | 1/12 | del 01/99. OED 201 12/02 |
| 24 | T224 JND | Scania L94 ib 4x2 | 1833717 | Irizar InterCentury | 150320 | C55F | 1999 | 5/99 | 12/18 | del 01/99. ASV 764 12/02-9/11 |
| 41 | GDZ 3841 | Leyland Leopard PSU3B/4R | 7500796 | Willowbrook Warrior (1990) | 88028 | B51F | 1975 | 9/99 | c01/00 | Ex Mayne, Manchester |
| 70 | TKU 540 | Leyland Tiger TRCTL11/3R | 8201498 | Plaxton Paramount 3500 | 8312LTH1C869 | C49Ft | 1983 | 10/99 | 9/01 | Ex Mayne (A370 HNC) |
| 69 | SSV 269 | Leyland Tiger TRCTL11/3R | 8200487 | Plaxton Paramount 3500 Exp | 8312LTH1X503 | C55F | 1983 | 1/00 | ?? | Ex Mayne (ANA 368Y) |
| 54 | ASV 764 | Leyland Leopard PSU5/4R (TL11) | 7102233 | Duple 320 (10/86) | 8590/0007 | C57F | 1973 | 1/00 | 1/03 | Was ORO 325L with VH body. Became RFM 299L 12/02, then MJI 5765 1/03. Later C70F |
| 27 | W427 JBU | Volvo B7R-63 | 000162 | Plaxton Prima | 9912TCM1372 | C55F | 2000 | 3/00 | 4/06 |  |

| Fleet No | Reg. No | Chassis | Number | Bodywork | Number | Capacity* | New | In | Out | Notes |
|---|---|---|---|---|---|---|---|---|---|---|
| 28 | W428 JBU | Volvo B7R-63 | 001437 | Plaxton Prima | 9912TCM1375 | C55F | 2000 | 3/00 | 4/06 | |
| 25 | W425 JBU | Volvo B10M-62 | 061327 | Plaxton Premiere 320 | 9912VUM1169 | C55F | 2000 | 4/00 | by 10/19 | Became M4 YNF 3/03-11/17. Later C70F |
| 26 | W426 JBU | Volvo B10M-62 | 061328 | Plaxton Premiere 320 | 9912VUM1170 | C55F | 2000 | 4/00 | ?/21 | Became M4 YNC 4/05, then NMX 643 9/07. Later C70F |
| 6 | NIL 8256 | Leyland Atlantean AN68B/1R | 8101879 | Northern Counties | 2208 | H43/32F | 1982 | 8/00 | 2/03 | Ex Mayne, M/cr (32). Became SND 483X again 2/03 |
| 8 | NIL 8258 | Leyland Atlantean AN68B/1R | 8100966 | Northern Counties | 2136 | H43/32F | 1981 | 8/00 | 9/03 | Ex Mayne, Manchester (38). Previously SND 425X |
| | BVR 100T | Leyland Fleetline FE30AGR | 7804945 | Northern Counties | 8604 | H43/32F | 1979 | 7/01 | c11/02 | Ex Mayne, Manchester (36) |
| 21 | A101 DPB | Dennis Falcon HS SDA407 | 142 | WS Vanguard (1987) | 1840/87 | DP49F | 1983 | 7/01 | c4/04 | Ex Mayne, M/cr (21). In use 9/01. Wdn after accident |
| | KDB 137V | Leyland Fleetline FE30AGR | 7805990 | Northern Counties | 8847 | H43/32F | 1980 | 7/01 | c12/02 | Ex Mayne, Manchester (37) |
| (r) | MJI 5766 | Leyland Leopard PSU3F/4R | 7930019 | Plaxton Supreme IV Express | 8011LX584 | C53F | 1980 | 8/01 | c6/06 | Ex Mayne, Manchester (66). Originally MRJ 358W |
| 10 | C110 UBC | Scania N112DRB | 1809026 | East Lancs | A6601 | H46/33F | 1986 | 5/02 | 01/04 | Ex Mayne, Manchester (20) |
| 11 | C111 UBC | Scania N112DRB | 1809027 | East Lancs | A6602 | H46/33F | 1986 | 5/02 | by 11/12 | Ex Mayne, Manchester (21). Became NIL 8256 2/03 |
| 12 | C112 UBC | Scania N112DRB | 1809028 | East Lancs | A6603 | H46/33F | 1986 | 5/02 | 7/09 | Ex Mayne, Manchester (22) |
| 13 | C113 UBC | Scania N112DRB | 1809029 | East Lancs | A6604 | H46/33F | 1986 | 5/02 | 7/09 | Ex Mayne, Manchester (23). Became NIB 4162 9/06 |
| 79 | LIB 6439 | Leyland Tiger TRCTLXCT/3RZ | 8401076 | Plaxton Paramount 3200II | 8512LGP2C001 | C55F | 1985 | 7/02 | by 5/12 | Ex Mayne, Manchester (79). Ex C57F and B649 RNA |
| 5 | IAZ 4775 | Leyland Fleetline FE30AGR | 7806339 | Northern Counties | 8905 | H43/32F | 1980 | 11/02 | by 12/07 | Ex Mayne (5/35). MNC 487W from 4/04. Withdrawn 9/05. Last Mayne Fleetline |
| 7 | IAZ 4776 | Leyland Fleetline FE30AGR | 7806266 | Northern Counties | 8906 | H43/32F | 1980 | 11/02 | 10/06 | Ex Mayne, Manchester (6/36). Withdrawn 9/05 |
| 29 | YS03 ZHZ | Scania K114IB | 1844762 | Irizar InterCentury 12.32 | 151182 | C55F | 2003 | 6/03 | by 2/20 | Became SSV 269 in ?? |
| 30 | YN03 DDK | Scania K114IB | 1844643 | Irizar InterCentury 12.32 | 151181 | C55F | 2003 | 6/03 | by 2/20 | del 4/03. 403 BGO from 10/08. |
| 18 | N512 MPN | Volvo B10M-62 | 043870 | Plaxton Premiere 350 | 9512VUP4331 | C49Ft | 1995 | 3/04 | 7/15 | Ex Brighton & Hove (512) via Mayne 3/04. Became HJZ 1918 6/04-7/15 |
| 31 | YN04 AFX | Scania K114IB | 1847075 | Irizar InterCentury 12.32 | 151406 | C55F | 2004 | 5/04 | ?/21 | Became UCE 665 in ?? |
| 32 | YN04 AFY | Scania K114IB | 1847254 | Irizar InterCentury 12.32 | 151407 | C55F | 2004 | 5/04 | ?/20 | Became NIB 4162 10/09. Struck low bridge 19/9/19, later scrapped |
| 14 | E704 EFG | Scania N112DRB | 1813192 | East Lancs | A8404 | H47/33F | 1988 | 9/05 | 1/11? | Ex Mayne, Manchester (21) |
| 33 | RJI 8684 | Bova FHD12-290 | 4112 | Bova Futura | | C49Ft | 1989 | 9/05 | By /11 | Ex Johnson, Henley-in-Arden (F260 NUT) |
| 34 | B18 JCT | Bova FHD12-290 | 3003847 | Bova Futura | | C49Ft | 1987 | 10/05 | by 11/11 | Ex Johnson, Henley-in-Arden (E871 TUA) |
| 36 | YN06 JXG | Scania K114IB4 | 1853872 | Irizar InterCentury Capacity | 151610 | C55F | 2006 | 4/06 | 3/14? | |
| 37 | YN06 JXH | Scania K114IB4 | 1853881 | Irizar InterCentury Capacity | 151611 | C55F | 2006 | 4/06 | 7/14 | |
| 35 | YN06 JXF | Scania K114IB4 | 1853621 | Irizar InterCentury Capacity | 151609 | C55F | 2006 | 4/06 | ?/21 | |
| 15 | E709 EFG | Scania N112DRB | 1813650 | East Lancs | A8409 | H47/33F | 1988 | 9/07 | 1/11 | Ex Mayne (5). |
| 27 | YN57 BWX | Alexander Dennis Javelin SFD745 | BR55GJ22598 | Plaxton Profile C | 0712GRX7306 | C55F | 2007 | 9/07 | 2/22 | Became LIB 6437 by 7/16 |
| 28 | YN57 BWY | Alexander Dennis Javelin SFD745 | BR55GJ22588 | Plaxton Profile C | 0712GRX7311 | C55F | 2007 | 9/07 | 2/22 | Became MA06 YNE in 11/18 |
| 51 | YS02 XDW | Scania K114IB | 1842253 | Irizar Century | 150960 | C55F | 2002 | 10/07 | 6/16 | Became RAZ 5171 by 11/10 |
| 52 | YS02 XDX | Scania K114IB | 1842642 | Irizar Century | 150961 | C55F | 2002 | 10/07 | 6/16 | Became NIL 9774 in 1/09 |
| 53 | YN03 WRW | Scania K114IB | 1844638 | Irizar Century | 151180 | C55F | 2003 | 10/07 | 6/16 | Became HIG 3853 by 9/10 |

| Fleet No | Reg. No | Chassis | Number | Bodywork | Number | Capacity* | New | In | Out | Notes |
|---|---|---|---|---|---|---|---|---|---|---|
| 56 | SIL 3856 | Bova FLC12.290 XL9AA12NGT | 6063631 | Bova Futura Club | | C55F | 1996 | 10/07 | 8/11 | Originally N56 CNF |
| 57 | LIB 6437 | Bova FHD12-340 | 7003501 | Bova Futura | | C49Ft | 1998 | 10/07 | 11/14 | Originally S57 TNA |
| 58 | NIL 8258 | Bova FHD12-340 | 7003511 | Bova Futura | | C49Ft | 1998 | 10/07 | 10/14 | Originally T58 JDB |
| 59 | YN04 GPZ | Scania K124IB4 | 1847486 | Irizar PB | 101568 | C49Ft | 2004 | 10/07 | 8/10? | Became PJZ 2159 by 7/10 |
| 60 | RIL 8160 | Volvo B10M-60 | 24804 | Plaxton Paramount 3500IV | 9012VCB2047 | C46Ft | 1992 | 10/07 | 10/14 | Originally J247 TFP. Wdn 3/09 |
| 63/75 | TKU 540 | Scania L94 ib 4x2 | 1833095 | Irizar InterCentury | 150279 | C55F | 1998 | 10/07 | 11/14 | Originally S63 TNA |
| 64/30 | 403 BGO | Scania L94 ib 4x2 | 1833136 | Irizar InterCentury | 150272 | C55F | 1998 | 10/07 | 10/08? | Originally T64 JDB |
| 67 | BIG 4667 | Dennis Javelin 12SDA2155 | 1465 | UVG Unistar | 5104/96 | C55F | 1996 | 10/07 | /17 | Ex N67 YVR & C55F 5/06 |
| 71 | RAZ 5171 | Dennis Javelin 11SDL2133 | 890 | Plaxton | 9311HZM1452 | C49F | 1993 | 10/07 | -/08? | L148 BFV & C47F to 4/04 |
| 74 | NIL 9774 | Dennis Javelin 11SDL2133 | 929 | Plaxton | 9311HZM1467 | C49F | 1994 | 10/07 | -/08? | L107 SDY & C47F to 4/04 |
| 75 | IAZ 4775 | Dennis Javelin 11SDL2133 | 923 | Plaxton | 9311HZM1463 | C49F | 1994 | 10/07 | -/08? | L102 SDY & C47F to 4/04 |
| 76 | IAZ 4776 | Scania L94 | 1833137 | Irizar InterCentury | 150278 | C50Ft | 1998 | 10/07 | 11/14 | Originally T65 JDB |
| 81 | W81 JBN | Volvo B7R-73 | 000141 | Plaxton Prima | 9812VLM7791 | C55F | 1999 | 10/07 | by 6/10 | |
| 68 | BIG 4668 | Dennis Javelin 12SDA2155 | 1466 | UVG Unistar | 5105/96 | C55F | 1996 | 10/07 | ?? | N68 YVR & C55F to 6/06 |
| 83 | W83 JBN | Volvo B7R-73 | 001431 | Plaxton Prima | 9912TCM1663 | C55F | 1999 | 10/07 | ?? | |
| 78 | EUK 978 | Volvo B10M | YV31MA618VAO46306 | Plaxton Premiere 320 | 12VUN6040 | C55F | 1997 | 10/07 | by 2/20 | Originally P76 JND. Later C70F del 1/09. Became M4 YNC in ? |
| 60 | YT09 FMA | Scania K340IB4 | 1861090 | Irizar PB | 160158 | C49Ft | 2009 | 3/09 | 12/12 | Became MA54 YNE by 2/20 |
| 54 | YT09 FMC | Scania K310IB4 | 1861039 | Irizar i4 | 160159 | C59F | 2009 | 3/09 | 2/22 | |
| 55 | YT09 FMD | Scania K310IB4 | 1861019 | Irizar i4 | 160160 | C59F | 2009 | 3/09 | 2/22 | |
| 62 | YT59 NZJ | Scania K310IB4 | 1865418 | Irizar i4 | 160723 | C59F | 2009 | 9/09 | 2/22 | Became MA57 YNE in 11/18 |
| 61/20 | YT59 NZK | Scania K310IB4 | 1865445 | Irizar i4 | 160724 | C59F | 2009 | 9/09 | 2/22 | Became MA56 YNE in 11/18 |
| 59 | YT60 OSM | Scania K360EB4 | 1869704 | Lahden Scania OmniCity Exp | 8106 | C55F | 2010 | 9/10 | 2/22 | Became SBM 9 in 9/12, then MA59 YNE in 11/18 |
| 56 | YT60 OSN | Scania K360EB4 | 1869715 | Lahden Scania OmniCity Exp | 8107 | C55F | 2010 | 9/10 | 4/18 | Withdrawn after engine fire |
| 63 | YT11 LRF | Scania K320IB4 | YS2K4X2000186728... | Irizar i4 | 160204 | C59F | 2011 | 3/11 | 2/22 | Became MA60 YNE in 11/18 |
| 17 | YN05 WJU | Scania K114IB4 | 1849167 | Irizar PB | 102547 | C49Ft | 2005 | 8/11 | by 10/19 | Ex Veolia. OED 201 from 1/12 |
| 19 | P959 YGG | Volvo B10M-62 | YV31M2B14TA044075 | Plaxton Premiere | 9512VUP4470 | C49Ft | 1997 | 8/11 | 8/15 | Ex Rossendale. JIG 6619 8/11-7/15 |
| 20 | P958 YGG | Volvo B10M-62 | YV31M2B18TA044077 | Plaxton Premiere | 9512VUP4472 | C49Ft | 1997 | 8/11 | 8/15 | Ex Rossendale. JIG 6620 in 8/11-7/15 |
| 64 | YN04 GPK | Scania K114IB4 | 1848308 | Irizar PB | 101699 | C49Ft | 2004 | 8/11 | c8/15 | Ex Veolia. DRZ 1364 8/11 |
| 65 | YN04 GKP | Scania K114IB4 | 1848198 | Irizar PB | 101690 | C49Ft | 2004 | 8/11 | by 10/19 | Ex Veolia. JIG 4365 8/11 |
| 66 | YN04 GKY | Scania K114IB4 | 1848246 | Irizar PB | 101694 | C49Ft | 2004 | 8/11 | by 10/19 | Ex Veolia. JIG 4366 8/11 |
| 11 | S961 YOO | Volvo Olympian 50 | 29125 | Alexander Belfast RH | 9733/3 | H47/31F | 1998 | 8/11 | ?/21 | Ex Dublin Bus 98-D-20416 (RV416). Cvtd H47/22D |
| | YT62 JCJ | Scania K400EB (tri-axle) | YS2K6X20001876664 | Irizar PB | 106216 | C53Ft | 2012 | 10/12 | 11/15 | |
| 14 | YX14 SEY | Volvo B9R | YV3S5P721EA164838 | Plaxton Elite | DE07/01 | C49-53Flt | 2014 | 3/14 | 2/22 | Became 3795D in 7/15 & MA14 YNE in 4/19 |
| 23 | J26 JHT | Leyland Olympian | ON20309 | Alexander RH | 1991/4 | H57/45F | 1992 | 5/14 | ?/21 | Ex Moreton, Chineham. New to China Light & Power, Hong Kong (FN 712) |
| 33 | YM09 TOH | Volvo B9R | YV3S5M1298A129007 | Plaxton Panther 2 | 0812 3TFR7949 | C53F | 2009 | 10/14 | 2/22 | Ex Matthews, Inniskeen (09MN590). Became IAZ 4776 11/14, then MA53 YNE by 2/20 |
| 34 | YM59 SVW | Volvo E9R | YV3S5P726AA136768 | Plaxton Panther 2 | 0912 3TFR8250 | C53F | 2010 | 10/14 | 2/22 | Ex Matthews, Inniskeen (10MN271). TKU 540 from 11/14 |
| 15 | YX64 WBO | Volvo B11R | YV3T2U824EA165671 | Plaxton Panther 3 | EP11/01 | C53Ft | 2014 | 12/14 | 2/22 | Became C2 SBM in ?? |
| 16 | YX15 ZBN | Volvo B8R | YV3T7U525FA170885 | Plaxton Leopard | EL39/01 | C59F | 2015 | 4/15 | 2/22 | Became MA08 YNE in 11/18 |

| Fleet No | Reg. No | Chassis | Number | Bodywork | Number | Capacity* | New | In | Out | Notes |
|---|---|---|---|---|---|---|---|---|---|---|
| 18 | YX65 ZHV | Volvo B8R | YV3S5P726AA136768 | Plaxton Leopard | FL04/01 | C72F | 2015 | 9/15 | 2/22 | Became MA58 YNE in 11/18 |
| 19 | YY65 SYC | Volvo B8R | YV3T7U52XGA174271 | Plaxton Leopard | FL06/01 | C72F | 2015 | 11/15 | 2/22 | Became MA03 YNE in 11/18 |
| 12 | YX66 WNC | Volvo B8R | YV3T7U520GA179284 | Plaxton Leopard | GL06/01 | C72F | 2016 | 9/16 | 2/22 | Became MA53 YNE in 11/18, then MA12 YNE by 2/20 |
| 21 | YX66 WND | Volvo B8R | YV3T7U524GA179286 | Plaxton Leopard | GL07/01 | C72F | 2016 | 9/16 | 2/22 | Became MA61 YNE in 11/18 |
| 61 | YJ08 EAK | VH TD921A | YE2921SU339D52946 | Van Hool Altano | 52946 | CH52/3Flt | 2008 | 10/17 | 2/22 | Ex Eavesway. Became M4 YNF in 11/17 |
| 60 | YJ10 DFD | VH TD921A | YE2921SU351D53274 | Van Hool Altano | 53274 | CH52/5Flt | 2010 | 4/18 | 2/22 | Ex Eavesway. Became MA09 YNE in 9/18 |
| 10 | YX18 LLN | Volvo B8R | YV3T7U522JA188107 | Plaxton Leopard | HL15/01 | C72F | 2018 | 5/18 | 2/22 | Later MA10 YNE by 2/20 |
| 24 | YX18 LLM | Volvo B8R | YV3T7U527JA189625 | Plaxton Leopard | HL29/01 | C72F | 2018 | 5/18 | 2/22 | |
| 17 | SD60 KHP | Volvo B9R | YV3S5P722BA144335 | Plaxton Elite | 1012.6SAA8730 | C70FI | 2011 | 10/19 | 2/22 | Ex Parks, Hamilton (HSK 645), C48Flt. Red livery |
| 22 | SD60 DGY | Volvo B9R | YV3S5P729BA144137 | Plaxton Elite | 1012.6SAA8724 | C70FI | 2011 | 10/19 | 2/22 | Ex Parks, Hamilton (KSK 952), C48Flt. Cream livery |
| 25 | SD60 DGX | Volvo B9R | YV3S5P726BA144287 | Plaxton Elite | 1012.6SAA8729 | C70FI | 2011 | 10/19 | 2/22 | Ex Parks, Hamilton (HSK 644), C48Flt. Cream livery |

*KEY:
B - Single-deck bus
C - Coach
CH - Double-deck coach seats
DP - Dual Purpose bus
H - Double-deck bus
M - minivan; the numbers denote the seats (upper/lower deck) and the last letter denotes the entrance position - Front, Centre, Dual or Rear
I - indicates a coach fitted with a wheelchair lift
t - an executive coach fitted with a washroom and servery

This Alexander Belfast-bodied Volvo Olympian was new to Dublin Bus in 1998. It was imported to the UK and converted from a dual-door layout in 2011 and put to use on school work for Mayne at Warrington. It later moved to the Manchester yard on a temporary basis to provide one of the shuttle services to Bury College. Dennis Javelin number 68 is seen in the background. *(BL)*